Body Music

Body Music

DENNIS LEE

Anansi

This edition published in 1998 by
House of Anansi Press Limited
34 Lesmill Road
Toronto, Ontario M3B 2T6
Tel. (416) 445-3333
Fax (416) 445-5967
E-mail Customer.Service@ccmailgw.genpub.com

02 01 00 99 98   1 2 3 4 5

CANADIAN CATALOGUING IN PUBLICATION DATA
Lee, Dennis, 1939-
Body music
ISBN 0-88784-627-0

1. Canadian Literature (English) – 20th century – History and criticism.*
2. Authors, Canadian (English) – 20th century.* I. Title.

PS8523.E3B62 1998   C810.9'0054   C98-931782-X
PR9199.3.I.387B62 1998

Cover design: Bill Douglas @ The Bang
Typesetting: ECW Type & Art, Oakville

Printed and bound in Canada

*House of Anansi Press gratefully acknowledges the
Canada Council for the Arts and the Ontario Arts
Council for their support of our publishing program.*

Contents

Preface vii

PART ONE

Cadence, Country, Silence 3
Roots and Play 27
Polyphony 51

PART TWO

The Poetry of Al Purdy 73
Acts of Dwelling, Acts of Love 103
Judy Merril Meets Rochdale College 111
Memories of Miron 119
Grant's Impasse 129

PART THREE

The Luminous Tumult 163
Poetry and Unknowing 179
Body Music 197

Notes on the Text 229

Preface

From time to time as I worked on this book, friends would ask what it was about. I found myself at a loss. Was it a work of literary criticism? Well, yes, but no. A theory of poetry? I hoped not. Did it belong under Canadian studies? Philosophy? Literary memoirs? Spiritual formation? Each of those categories was relevant, but none was on the mark. To say what the essays were reaching for, I needed a broader context.

In a particular sense of the word, these are stories. Tales from a life. Yarns of experience. The notion may seem far-fetched, since there is little anecdotal detail. But let me suggest, by a roundabout route, why it feels appropriate.

*

There are certain things that speak to us at the core, but that scarcely exist within the assumptions of modern thought. I have in mind the kind of reality people once pointed to with terms like "good," "evil," "the sacred."

It is not that we have lost contact with such things in our lives, but rather that educated thinking no longer recognizes them as having any substance. Over the last few centuries, our traditional languages of meaning have largely faded; they seemed passé in the world described by science. And the language of fact that superseded them has no place for evil or beauty — except as subjective "values," which we project onto a neutral universe. This account of facts and values is taken for granted in most modern thought; we have trouble thinking about things that matter without adopting its assumptions.

But while it puts an end to a good deal of superstition, the account gets less and less satisfactory when you try to shoehorn your actual experience into it. For one thing, it declares that our deepest leadings and toughest moral dilemmas are no more substantial than our tastes in hobbies or hairstyles. Again, it trivializes actions which are clearly beyond the pale, like torture or genocide. I may call them evil, but someone else can call them good; since all value judgements are subjective, we could decide which one to choose by flipping a coin. And eventually the theory undermines itself. In the name of adhering to truth, it is forced to deny that we have any obligation *to* adhere to truth — since it does not accept that such objective obligations exist in the first place.

Mind you, very few of us actually live as if all this were so. We find ourselves tugged back and forth, sometimes painfully, by stubborn realities that don't even have names within this account. Yet however we respond to those tugs, the situation is the same. What we know by living our lives, and what we can think within the categories of educated discourse, are no longer on speaking terms.

This is a sorry state for a civilization to be in. We need a more sophisticated form of thinking: one that can deal with both fact and meaning, proceed with rigour and awe at once. But that won't materialize overnight. And until it does, it seems to me, it's worthwhile just sitting still. Swapping stories of what does claim us, even if we have no concepts in which to formulate it. Like travellers in unmapped territory, exchanging descriptions of the landmarks they've discovered. For these experiences of being claimed *are* among our landmarks — basic givens, which a more adequate way of thinking would ponder and sift, and eventually orient itself by.

How are we seized by what we cannot bargain with? What do we know for real? A poet's experience gives only part of the answer, of course. We also need to hear what a parent knows firsthand, and a physicist, and a factory worker. That said, the meditations that follow are one man's response to the questions. They tell stories of what has claimed me in practising my craft, and in drawing nourishment from other people's words. They speak of the things I live by as a poet.

★

The essays were written between 1972 and 1998. All have been revised in the last two years, though most retain their original perspective and references. The sequence is chronological, with minor detours; dates of original publication appear in the notes at the end.

Many of my mentors are long dead. Only a few are named, but I presume my debts will be evident. Let me also thank the friends who have helped me clarify my hunches, often by strenuous disagreement. They include Phil Balsam, Donna Bennett, Roo Borson, Michael Boughn, Robert Bringhurst, Russell Brown, William Christian, Matt Cohen, Arthur Davis, Stan Dragland, Lon Dubinsky, Sheila Fischman, David Gilmour, Sheila Grant, Eamon Grennan, Wendy Lesser, Tim Lilburn, Kim Maltman, Don McKay, Linda McKnight, Andy Miller, Eric Miller, George Payerle, my wife Susan Perly, Zdravko Planinc, John Porter, Michael Redhill, Margaret Roffey, my editor Martha Sharpe, Peter Turner, Jan Zwicky. I owe a particular debt to Sean Kane, who over the years has commented on many drafts of these essays with attentiveness and grace.

PART ONE

Cadence, Country, Silence

Writing in Colonial Space

What am I doing when I write?

I don't know.

A hockey player may understand very little about the principles of anatomy. But he gets his body across the ice somehow.

What am I doing when I write? The question is too important to discuss at a writers' conference, even this one. It is posed by the writing that wants to be done. And it is answered, sometimes, by the writing *as* it is done. There's not much left over to analyze what is going on.

Still, it's possible to make companionable noises — like when you're helping to lift a heavy crate, enjoying music, making love.

1. *Cadence*

Most of my time as a poet is spent listening into a luminous tumble, a sort of taut cascade. I call it "cadence." If I withdraw from immediate contact with things around me, I can sense it churning, flickering, thrumming, locating things in more shapely relation to one another. It feels continuous, though I may spend days on end without noticing it.

What I hear is initially without words. But when a poem starts to come, the words have to accord with that energy or I can't make the poem at all. (I speak of "hearing" cadence, but the sensation isn't auditory. It's more like sensing a constantly changing tremor with your body: a play of movement and stress, torsion and flex — as with the kinaesthetic perception of the muscles.) More and more I sense this energy as presence, both outside and inside myself, teeming toward words.

What *is* it?

I could give one kind of answer by pointing to a poem I've written, saying, "Feel how the poem moves here, and here; no, feel the deeper music in which it's sustained." But that wouldn't do. The rhythm of what I've written is such a small and often mangled fraction of what I sense, it tunes out so many wavelengths of that massive, infinitely fragile polyphony, that I almost despair. And if I try to define it conceptually, it's equally futile. Whatever categories I use seem to turn the indelible *thrum* into something abstract or theoretical — which is precisely what it isn't. I may not know what cadence is, but I know one thing: it is no more theoretical than breathing.

Nor can I say whether other writers respond to its prod. When I recognize traces in other people's work, it's more often in music and sculpture than in poetry. Though strongly in Pindar and Hölderlin. As in the Unaccompanied Cello Suites, Charlie Parker, Van Morrison. Or in Henry Moore, Jackson Pollock, Clyfford Still.

I take my vocation to consist of listening into this energy — for a time it was like the fusion of a burnished cello with a raunchy sax, but lately there have been organ and flute as well — I take my vocation to consist of listening into cadence with enough life concentration that it can become words through me if it chooses.

★

What is the relation of cadence and poem?

Michelangelo said he could sense the figure in the uncut stone; his job was to chip away marble till it emerged. Inuit sculptors say the same thing. And that makes sense to me. Cadence is the medium, the raw stone; the poem is already sustained in it. And writing means cutting away everything that isn't the poem. You can't "write" a poem, in fact — you can only help it stand free in the torrent. Most of my time with a pen is spent giving words, images, bright ideas that are borne along in cadence their permission to stay off the page. The poem is what remains; it is local cadence minus whatever is extraneous to its shapely articulation.

A bad poem, on the other hand, is something a poet made up.

This is why a poem, in my sense of it, wants to exist in two ways at once. As a teeming process which overflows every prior canon of form (or is prepared to, and can when it chooses). And simultaneously as a beautifully disciplined structure, whose order flowers outward from the centre of its own necessity, and doesn't miss a single checkpoint along the way. Cadence, which is the medium of existence for the content all along — cadence teems. Content has the other task, of filling out the orderly formal space of its local being. And those two ways — the energy of unlimited process, and the shapeliness of content living outward to the limit of its measure — have been coinciding all along. If the poem is any good they will go on coinciding within it; it will be intelligible out of courtesy, not timidity. Its form is not to obey form, but to include and carry beyond it.

In the presence of cadence — which feels continuous, as goad and grace and as something I experience almost as mockery — the chance to turn a good phrase, make up a deft poem, the chance to be "a poet," leaves me cold. It seems like the cheapest evasion. For this jazzy, majestic, delicately cascading process I hear surging and thudding and pausing is largely without the witness I might be, if it chose to animate my words.

I don't say that with any false humility, for I am convinced that it does so choose. But it impresses me with the dumbness of most of what a writer is tempted to do, and it leaves me impatient that I can't organize my life so as to listen with greater concentration. For finally, I believe, cadence chooses to issue in the articulate gestures of being.

*

What does cadence feel like?

Imagine you're sitting indoors. Down in the basement, a group with a heavily amplified bass is rehearsing. Nothing is audible, but the pulsating of the bass starts to make the girders and beams vibrate. And eventually the vibration makes its way into your body. You feel yourself being flexed by a tremor which you're bound to acknowledge, whether or not you know what it is.

That sensation is disorienting, because it collapses our familiar categories of inner and outer, subject and object. You don't perceive a vibration; *you vibrate*. Your muscular system has become both the recording instrument and the thing recorded. And the pulse you feel is neither subjective nor objective. Rather, it is your immediate portion of the kinaesthetic space in which you exist.

During my twenties, I became aware of something comparable. It was not my body that was being flexed, or not primarily. It was my — what do I say? My imagination? my psyche? my spirit? I don't know the right term, but the experience was unmistakable. I was imbedded, as plainly as I was in the earth's atmosphere, in a space which was alive and volatile, and whose flexions governed the tension and pulse of my system. If I sat quietly, I would regularly become aware of this preverbal field of force.

That didn't jibe with anything I knew, but eventually it was too immediate to deny. The term I seized on for the insistent tremor was "cadence." And cadence — the direct experience of that energy, not my ideas about it — has shaped my writing since shortly after my first book appeared.

It had no specific content, or none to begin with. It was its own content, a rich symphony of clench and swooping pulsation. Nor could I get any conceptual distance on it; the resources with which I might have analyzed it were already being tweaked and yo-yoed themselves. Often I went for weeks with no apprehension of the process, which nonetheless felt as if it continued its delicate judder and carom and chug without me.

And my writing vocation was given. A poem was meant to enact what cadence had been doing all along. Not by describing it, but by reliving its muscular trajectories in words.

2. *Country*

I hope I haven't implied that I simply heard the words of cadence and wrote them down. The beginnings were far more hit-and-miss than that.

The catalyst was Friedrich Hölderlin. I discovered his poetry in my early twenties, in a German course, and it changed my sense of how words could move on the page. And shortly after that I started getting intimations of a music, not specifically his, which I could feel bucking and pausing somewhere beyond my range of hearing. But those nudgings of cadence didn't lead to anything concrete right away. My own apprentice poetry was stuck in a creakily traditional prosody, and I couldn't get beyond it.

In fact I spent seven years composing a sequence of sonnet variations, *Kingdom of Absence*. Listen to one of these pieces:

When I review my troop of scruffy selves
and count personae, when I hear the tramp
of brawling cells in whichway phalanx wheeling,
spun by every creak of the swivelling wind,

and when I see the sleek and shifty mind,
doing his pander, and the awkward-squad volitions
fresh from screwing with his fair daughters;
I flinch that I must answer their salute.

All my limping rabble, and the sparks
from gaudy captains filing into the sun:
crow meat. At the dark wood, in torpor,
I led my soldiers naked into gunfire.
Gouts of blood are splattered beneath the birches.
My hash is coming apart beneath the leaves.

7

So much is wrong here — the stagey extended metaphor, the overly conscious mix of high and low diction, the young man's knee-jerk despair — that a reader may not pick up on what appals me most. Which is the rhythm. Or more accurately, the whole way of *hearing* rhythm. This is an ear that no longer hears metrically — or not with subtlety and bite, as in the great tradition from Chaucer to Yeats. But neither has it discovered a different music in the dance of syllables. So it just thumps along, trapped in the latter-day decadence of the iambic pentameter line.

Almost as fatally, the larger rhythmic gestures by which the poem moves are out of synch with themselves. Whatever exploratory energy may be trapped here, it almost certainly doesn't want to proceed by retracing the sonnet's shapes of discovery. But it has taken refuge there, and the structure has become a straitjacket. No matter how many cosmetic liberties the poet may take.

It wasn't until the sequence was published that the dam gave way at last, and I connected with the cadence I'd been hearing for years.

*

I still remember the summer of 1967. I was twenty-seven. *Kingdom of Absence* had appeared. And almost at once, the music I'd sensed for so long came barging through.

The new voice sounded like this:

> It would be better maybe if we could stop loving the children
> and their delicate brawls, pelting across the square in tandem, deking
> from cover to cover in raucous celebration and they are never
> winded, bemusing us with the rites of our own
> gone childhood; if only they stopped
> mattering, the children, it might be possible, now
> while the square lies stunned by noon.
> What is real is fitful, and always the beautiful footholds
> crumble the moment I set my mind aside, though the world does
>   recur.

Better, I think, to avoid the scandal of being — the headlong
    particulars
which, as they lose their animal purchase
cease to endorse us, though the ignominious hankerings
go on; this induces the ache of things, and the lonesome ego
sets out once again dragging its lethal desires across the world,
which does not regard them . . .

I found myself scrambling night after night to keep up with
these long, hurtling lines. They were no longer clumping
through preset metrical patterns. Instead, they moved with a
periodic yet off-balance gait which seemed to emerge directly
from this cascade of energy (for which I had no name as yet).
I remember sitting up each night in a kind of dictation high
— both cowed and exhilarated by the rhythms that had taken
me over.

Soon the nightly runs coalesced into a full-dress meditative
sequence. It kept coming and coming, and the first version of
Civil Elegies appeared in 1968.

But then something bizarre happened. I dried. For the next
three years, I couldn't write a thing that worked. Twenty
words on a page would set me wincing at their palpable
stiffness and falsity. I still went into my study and fiddled, but
I wound up scrapping everything I wrote. And I had no notion
where the music had gone. The dry spell was as unexpected
as the breakthrough had been.

I have a better sense of it now. There was a longstanding
check on my pen, which returned shortly after cadence declared itself. Words had arrived, but words had already gone
dead. And so there were old dues still to be paid.

*

To get at this complex situation, I need to explore how
cadence can be blocked at deeper levels than the personal.
And for that, I need to start from its hereness, its local nature.
We never encounter cadence in the abstract; it is insistently
here and now. But if we live in space which is radically in

9

question for us, that makes our barest speaking problematic to itself. For voice does issue in part from civil space. And alienation in that space will enter and undercut our writing, make it recoil upon itself, become a problem to itself.

What does that mean? Writing "becomes a problem to itself" when it raises a vicious circle: when to write involves something that seems to make writing impossible. Contradictions in our civil belonging are one thing which has that effect, and I am struck by the subtle connections people here have drawn between words and their public space.

Abraham Yehoshuah spoke yesterday of writing in a divided language. In part, modern Hebrew is charged with religious connotations which go back millennia, but which some Israelis no longer accept. And in part it is brand new, without the grainy texture of a living language. New words, technical ones in particular, are regularly created *ex nihilo* to make modernity articulate in Israel. Thus contemporary Hebrew embodies the tensions of ancient and modern, sacred and profane, which tug at Israel itself. Using it well demands a provisional triumph of citizenship, a reconciliation of jostling civil currents at the level of words and phrases.

And Michèle Lalonde speaks of coming to verbal maturity in Quebec in a kind of linguistic no-man's-land, speaking a French one has been taught to despise, and a rag-tag-and-bobtail English fit only for the Pepsi billboards which denote one's servitude. In such a situation, writing must be carried out in a language that embodies the very experience — societal humiliation — which must be transcended in order to write. In Quebec, as in Israel, writing is a problem to itself at the level of diction.

For an English Canadian, exploring the obstructions to cadence means exploring the nature of colonial space.

Yet our civil alienation is not manifested so dramatically in language. The prime fact about my country now is that it has become an American client state. But we speak the same tongue as our new masters. Thus while our comfortable inauthenticity has many tangible monuments, from TIME to Imperial

Esso, the way it undercuts our writing is not so easy to discern — precisely because there are no conspicuous verbal battle-fields in which the takeover is visible. Nevertheless, many writers here know how the act of writing calls itself into question.

I won't linger on the more obvious aspects of the tidal wave. How almost none of the books on our paperback racks are our own, because the American-owned distributors refuse to carry them. How our filmmakers have to go to the States to seek distribution for Canada, and are usually turned down. How most of our prime-time TV is filled with Yankee programs; how Alberta schoolchildren are still learning that Abraham Lincoln was their country's greatest president.

Every one of these idiocies must change. But I want to get beyond the familiar litany, for there are dimensions of cultural colonialism which go deeper than specific abuses. This entails stepping back and exploring how, in a colony, the bare exercise of the imagination becomes a problem to itself.

★

Let me return to my early experience. I began writing about 1960, when I was twenty-one. My sense at the time was that I had access to a great many words: those of the British tradition, the American, and so far as anyone took it seriously, the Canadian. (When I speak of "words," I mean all the resources of the verbal imagination — from nouns and verbs to structures of plot and versions of the hero.) Yet at the same time those words seemed to lie in a random heap, which glittered with promise so long as I considered it in the mass, but within which each individual word went stiff, inert, was somehow clogged with sludge the moment I tried to move it into a poem. I could stir words, prod them, cram them into place. But there was no way I could speak them as my own.

Writers everywhere don't begin with an external, resistant language; something more was involved than just getting the hang of the medium during apprenticeship. In any case, after I'd published one book of poems and finished another,

I stopped being able to use words on paper at all. Everywhere around me — in England, America, even Canada — writers opened their mouths and words spilled out like crazy. But I just gagged. And looking back at my earlier writing, I felt as if I'd been fishing pretty beads out of a vat of crankcase oil and stringing them together. The words weren't limber or alive, or even mine.

★

Those of us who stumbled into this problem in the 1960s were suffering the recoil from something Canadians had learned profoundly after World War II — at least where I lived, in southern Ontario. To want to see one's life made articulate on paper, in movies, in songs: that was ridiculous, uppity. Canadians were by definition people who looked over the fence at America, unself-consciously learning from its comics, pop music, and television how to go about being alive. The disdainful amusement I and thousands like me felt for Canadian achievement in any field, especially those of the imagination, was a direct reflection of our sense of inferiority. And while we sneered at American mass culture, we could distance ourselves from it only by soaking up all the élite American culture we could get: Mailer and Fiedler and Baldwin, the Beats and the hip. And we fell all over ourselves putting down the Canadians. This was between 1955 and 1965.

And like intellectual sellouts everywhere, we were prepared to capitulate, not for a cut of the action, but simply on condition that we not be humiliated by being lumped with the rest of the natives. We were desperate to make that clear: we weren't like the rest. The fact that we would never meet the Americans we admired didn't cramp our style. We managed to feel inferior anyway, and we compensated like mad. We kept up with *Paris Review* and *Partisan*, shook our heads over how Senator McCarthy had perverted our best traditions; in some cases we went down to Washington to confront our power structure, and in all cases we agreed that the greatest blot on our racial history was the way we had treated the

Negroes. It boggles the imagination, but that was what we did
— it's how we *felt*. We weren't pretending, we were desperate.
And the idea that these things only confirmed our colonialism
would have made us laugh our continentalized heads off. We
weren't all that clear on colonialism to begin with, but if
anybody had it, it was our poor countrymen, the Canadians,
who in some unspecified way were still in thrall to England.
But we weren't colonials; hell, we could have held up our
heads in New York. Though it was a bit of a relief that no one
asked us to try.

My awakening from this condition was private, and extremely disorienting. It was touched off by the American
critique of America during the war in Vietnam. But it ended
up going much further. From that muddled process I remember a couple of months in 1965, after a teach-in at the
University of Toronto. It lasted a weekend, and as I followed
the long, dull speeches in the echoing cavern of Varsity Arena,
two things dawned on me. The first was that the American
government had been lying about the war on a colossal scale.
And the second was that the Canadian media, from which I'd
learned most of what I knew about Vietnam, were spreading
its lies.

I present these discoveries in all the crashing naiveté with
which they struck me then. Interestingly, while the first
revelation shocked me more at the time, it was the second
that gnawed at me during the ensuing months. I couldn't get
my mind around it. I did not believe that our newspapers or
television had been bought off directly by Washington. But
if it was not a case of paid corruption, the only reason for
cooperating in such a blatant deception — consciously or not
— was that they were colonial media, serving the interests of
the imperial rulers. Mind you, that kind of language made
me bridle; it conjured up images of five-hour harangues in
Havana and Peking, foreign frenzies of auto-hypnosis. I'd read
about *that* in the papers too. But no matter. It was the only
language that made sense of what was happening.

Even worse, I had to recognize that this imperial influence

13

was not confined to the media. It also included my head. More and more of the ideas I had, my assumptions, even the instinctive path of my feelings, seemed to have come north from the States unexamined. That had once been what I strove for. But now the whole thing had turned around, and I was jarred loose. After ten years of continentalizing my ass, what had I accomplished?

I was a colonial.

It was during this time that I began to find literary words impossible. I didn't know why. But writing had become a full-fledged problem to itself. It had grown into a search for authenticity, but all it could be was a symptom of inauthenticity. I could feel that with every nerve end in my body. And so for three years I shut up.

★

Though I hope not to over-dramatize this, it was when I read a series of essays by the philosopher George Grant that I began to comprehend what we were living inside. His analysis of "Canadian Fate and Imperialism," which I read in 1967 in *Canadian Dimension*, was the first that made any contact with my tenuous sense of living here — the first in which I recognized the words of our civil condition. My whole system had been coiling in on itself for want of them. As subsequent pieces appeared (they were collected in 1969 as *Technology and Empire*, the book of Grant's from which I learned most deeply), I realized that somehow it had happened. A man who knew this paralyzing condition firsthand was nonetheless using words authentically, from the centre of everything that had tied my tongue.

One central perception was that in refusing the American dream, our Loyalist forebears — the British Americans who came north after 1776 — were groping to reaffirm a classical European tradition, which taught that reverence is more fully human than conquest or mastery. That we are subject to sterner necessities than liberty and the pursuit of happiness — that we must respond, as best we can, to the demands of the good. And that our lives here have an organic continuity which can be ruptured only at the risk of making our condition worse; that any such change should be undertaken in fear and trembling. (Grant did not claim that all Hellenic and Christian societies lived up to those ideals, only that they understood themselves to be acting well or badly in their light.) I knew that the Loyalists were not a homogeneous group, and that many had come north for the main chance. Yet convictions like these demonstrably underlay many of their attitudes to Europe, to law, the land, indigenous peoples. Their refusal of America issued, in part, from a disagreement about what it meant to be human.

What the Loyalists were refusing was the doctrine of essential freedom, which in an argument of inspired simplicity Grant sees as the point of generation of technological civilization. That doctrine led to a view of everything but our naked wills — the new continent, native peoples, other nations, outer space, even our own bodies — as raw material, to be manipulated according to the urges of our desires and the dictates of our technology. But not only did this view of an unlimited freedom seem arrogant and suicidal; it also seemed wrong. For we are not radically free, in point of fact. And to act as if we are is to behave with lethal naiveté.

Mind you, this overstates what Grant finds in the Loyalists. In fact, he declares that the typical Loyalist was "straight Locke with a dash of Anglicanism"; the British tradition he held to had already broken with the classical understanding of the good. Loyalism was a gesture in the right direction, perhaps, but it never succeeded in being radically un-American. It did not have the resources to reconstitute modernity.

This undercutting of a past he would have liked to make exemplary is a characteristic moment in Grant's thought, and it reveals the central strength and contradiction of his work. He withdraws from the contemporary world, and judges it with passionate lucidity, by standing on a fixed point — which he then reveals to be no longer there. Or at the very least, to be no longer accessible to the modern mind. This way of

15

proceeding makes his thought difficult to live within, a fact which his own best work explores rigorously.

I found this account of being alive less indulgent than the liberal version that achieved its zenith in America, far closer to the way things are. Now there were terms in which to recognize that, as we began to criticize our new masters during the sixties, we were not just hoping to be better Americans than they, to dream their dream more humanely. Our dissent went as deep as it did because, obscurely, we did not want to be American at all. Their dream was wrong.

Before Grant, a person who'd grown up in as deeply colonized a decade as the fifties had no access to such a conscious refusal of America. Our tiresome beginnings had always been a source of embarrassed disdain to us: no revolution, no Wild West frontier, no six-gun heroes. As this was stood on its head, Grant gave us access to our native space.

But Grant is scarcely an apostle of public joy. By now, he says, we have replaced our forebears' tentative, dissenting space with a wholehearted American one. The sellout of Canada which has been consummated over the last few decades does not involve just natural resources or corporate takeovers, nor who will put the marionettes in Ottawa through their dance. It replaces one way of being human with another.

For the political and military rule of the United States, and the economic rule of its corporations, are merely the surface expression of modernity in the West. That modernity is also inward. It shapes the expression of our bodies' impulses, the way we build cities, what we do with our spare time. Always we are totally free agents, faced with a world which is raw material, a permanent incitement to technique. There is no court of appeal outside that circuit. And even though we can observe this worldview destroying the planet, that does not give us access to a different worldview.

Hence to dissent from liberal modernity is to fall silent, for we have no terms in which to speak that do not issue from the very space we are trying to speak against. We may sense "intimations of deprival" to which modernity is not open, but we can sense them only inarticulately. Grant explores this impasse with a clarity which induces vertigo.

I recognize all the bleakness for which he is often criticized. But only with my head. For months after I read Grant's essays, I felt a surge of release and exhilaration; to find one's tongue-tied sense of civil loss and bafflement given words at last, to hear one's inarticulate hunches out loud, because most immediate in the bloodstream — and not prettied up, and in prose like a fastidious groundswell — was to stand erect at last in one's own place.

I do not expect to spend my lifetime agreeing with George Grant. But in my experience, the sombre Canadian has enabled us to say for the first time where we are, who we are — to become articulate. That gift of speech is a staggering achievement. And in trying to comprehend the deeper ways in which writing is a problem to itself in Canada, I am bound to start with Grant.

★

We are getting closer to the centre of the tangle. Why did I dry?

The words I knew said Britain, and they said America. But they did not say my home. They were always and only about someone else's life. All the rich structures of language were available, but the currents that animated them were not native to the people who use the language here.

But the civil self seeks nourishment as much as the biological. And if everything it lays hold of is alien, it may protect itself in a visceral spasm of refusal. To take an immediate example: the words I used above — "language," "home," "here" — have no native charge. They convey only meanings in whose face we have been unable to find ourselves since the eighteenth century. This is not to call for arbitrary new Canadian definitions, of course. It is simply to point out that the texture, weight, and connotation of almost every word we use comes from abroad. For a person who wants to recreate our being human here in words — and where else do we live? — that creates an absolute impasse.

Why did I dry?

The language was drenched with our nonbelonging. And words — bizarre as it sounds, even to myself — words had become the enemy. To use them was to collaborate further in one's extinction as a rooted human being. And so by a drastic and involuntary stratagem of self-preserval, words went dead.

The first necessity for a colonial writer, so runs the conventional wisdom, is to write of what he knows. His imagination must come home. But that first necessity is not enough. For if you are Canadian, home is the place that is not home to you — it is even less your home than the imperial centre you've dreamt about. Or to say what I really know, the *words* of home are silent. And to raise a stirring classical ode to the harvests of Saskatchewan, or set an American murder mystery in Newfoundland is no answer at all. Try to speak the words of your home and you will discover, if you are a colonial, that you do not know them. You are left chafing at the inarticulacy of a native space that may not even exist. So you shut up.

But perhaps — and here was the breakthrough — perhaps our job was not to fake a space of our own and write it up, but rather to speak the words of our spacelessness. Perhaps that *was* home. This dawned on me gradually. Instead of pushing against the grain of an external, uncharged language, perhaps we should come to writing *with* that grain.

To do so was a homecoming — and a thoroughly iffy homecoming it was. You began by giving up the notion of writing in the same continuum as Lowell, Ginsberg, Olson, Plath, Hughes. Yet it was not a matter of taking an easier road; finding your own voice would be chancier than echoing theirs. Rather, it meant assuming that what is for real can be claimed by a Canadian in the language of his own time and place. If he can learn to speak that language. And so you began striving to hear what happened in words — in "love," "inhabit," "fail," "earth," "home" — as you let them surface in your mute and native land. This was an eerie, visceral process; there was nothing as explicit as starting to write in *joual*. There was only the decision to let words be how they are for us.

But I am distorting the experience again by writing it down. There was nothing conscious about this, initially at least; it was simply a direction one's inner ear took up. I know I fought it.

★

The first mark of words, as you began to re-hear them in this empty civil space, was a blur of unachieved meaning. That much I knew already. But the oppressiveness started to change, for I could sense something more.

Where I lived, a whole swarm of inarticulate meanings lunged, clawed, drifted, eddied, sprawled in half-grasped disarray beneath the tidy meaning which the simplest word brought with it from England and the States. "City": once you learned to accept the featureless character of that word — responding to it as a Canadian noun, with its absence of native connotation — you were dimly savaged by the live, inchoate meanings trying to surface through it. The whole tangle and Sisyphean problematic of people's existing here, from the time of the *coureurs de bois* to the present day, came struggling to be included in "city." Cooped up beneath the familiar surface of the word as we use it (city as Paris, London, New York) — and cooped up further down still, beneath the blank and blur you heard when you sought some received indigenous meaning — listening all the way down, you began to overhear the lives of millions of men and women who went their particular ways here, whose roots and legacy come together in the cities we live in. Halifax, Montreal, Toronto, Vancouver: "city" meant something still unspoken, but rampant with energy. Hearing it was like watching the contours of an unexpected continent declare themselves through the familiar lawns and faces of your block.

Though that again is hindsight. You heard an energy, and those lives were part of it. Under the surface alienation of our words, and under the second-level silence, there was a living barrage of meaning. Private, civil, religious — unclassifiable, finally, but teeming to be uttered. And I felt that press of meaning. I had no idea what it was, but I could sense it swarming toward words.

And buoyed by that energy, I started to write again.

⋆

Why does this tale of writing, falling silent for three years, beginning to write again, feel slightly foreign?

Because I barely recognize the protagonist, for one thing. The story implies a ten-year coherence of purpose — which I admire as I read. But what I actually felt during most of that decade was a sense of beleaguered drifting. And while it was punctuated with flashes of clarity, I'm mortified to report that they were usually at odds with one another.

Moreover, the chronology is awkward, uncooperative. The story implies a sequence that runs like this. Poet writes artificial early work; dissatisfied with its stiffness, he stops writing; George Grant's essays furnish an explanation for his block; as a result something called "cadence" happens to him, and he starts to write again.

That's easy to follow, and edifying. But in fact it went more like this. Poet writes artificial early work, while being haunted by a deeper music; after his first book appears, he connects with that cadence; meanwhile he's reading George Grant in dribs and drabs; for no discernible reason, he stops being able to write when the second book comes out; three years later, again with no obvious cause, he returns to that book and revises it.

How does it all fit together? There are so many loose ends, I've given up looking for a sequential logic. None of the causes and effects are in the right place. But even a thematic account of the process, which is what I've sketched in this essay, dramatizes and streamlines things that were much more tangled, murky, and banal as they occurred.

⋆

Those are reservations that need to be recognized. But they matter less than the experience that generates them.

20

One thing I find now is that I can write only from the promptings of cadence. And being a colonial, I find they surface mainly when I hunker into the muteness of words. I can no more observe something in the street, go home, and write it up than I can fly.

So it will not do to ignore our halting tongues and simply write of other things; nor to spend all our energy castigating the external causes, as if the colonial condition were wholly outside us; nor to invert that tongue-tied estate and fake a passionate cascade of words, as if we could will ourselves to be everything we are not. The impasse of writing that is problematic to itself is transcended only when the impasse becomes its own subject, when writing accepts and enters and names its own condition as it names the world. Any other course (except in deliberately minor work — though I don't put that down) leads to writing whose joints and musculature don't work together.

To name your colonial condition is not necessarily to assign explicit terms to it. It may be, as in the poetry of Milton Acorn or Gaston Miron. But the weight of the silence can also be conveyed by the sheer pressure behind the words that finally break it. Then to name one's condition is to recreate the halt and stammer, the wry self-deprecation, the rush of celebratory elan and the vastness of the still unspoken surround in which a colonial writer comes to know his house, his father, her city and land — encounters them in their own unuttered terms, and finds words being born to speak them. I think of Al Purdy's poems.

Beneath the words our absentee masters have given us, there is an undermining silence. It saps our nerve. And beneath that silence, there is a raw welter of cadence that tumbles and strains toward words. It makes the silence a blessing, because it shushes easy speech. That cadence is home.

We do not own cadence. It is not in Canada; Canada is in it, along with everything else. Nor is it real only for colonials. But it has its own way of speaking our lives, if we are willing to be struck dumb. And through us, it seeks to issue in the articulate gestures of being. Here.

3. *Silence*

What are these gestures?

In one session of this conference, Claude Vigée spoke of the stillness, even the death, which one must reenter before words can be spoken. The void underlies each syllable, and affords its perpetual context. And many of the hallowed terms of the century were invoked to echo that silence: nothingness, the abyss, nonbeing, meaninglessness.

But Abraham Yehoshuah disagreed. No writer starts with an experience of void. You begin with a character, a situation, a snatch of rhythm — some concrete thing that grabs you. That sets the project: to make the story or poem. And once you write it, it's written. What part does the void play in that? It is simply mumbo jumbo, called in for its fashionable aura of spiritual extremis.

Notice that the disagreement is not between abstract theories of literature. It arose when two practising writers described the daily act of putting words on paper. Their workaday experience is diametrically opposed, or at least their accounts of it are.

I find myself in agreement with both accounts. A good piece of writing bespeaks encounter with emptiness as its source; a good piece of writing bespeaks encounter with things, things as they are, nothing but things alive with their own thingness, as its source. What's more, I'm convinced that both accounts must be true of any piece of writing — and simultaneously — or it will degenerate into portentousness or banality.

★

There is a moment in which I experience other people, situations, things as standing forth with a clarity and a preciousness that make me want to cry and to celebrate physically at the same time. I imagine many people have felt it.

It is the moment in which something becomes overwhelmingly real in two lights at once. An old person whose will to live and whose mortality reach me at the same instant. A child who is coursed through with the lovely energies of its body, and yet is totally fragile before the coming decades of its life. A social movement charged with a passion for decent lives, and at the same time with the egotism and shrillness that will debase it. A table, at once a well-worn companion and a disregarded adjunct. Each stands forth as what it is most fully, and most preciously, because the emptiness in which it rests declares itself so overpoweringly. We realize that this thing or person, this phrase, this event *need not be.* And at that moment it reveals its vivacious being as though it had just begun to exist.

The recognition itself is "subjective," I suppose; it is we who change at that moment. But the double situation of the child, the table, the social movement is already a given; its life and its death are simultaneous, whether we recognize that or not. The fact that we can be open to it only rarely does not change this coincidence of what is with its own nonbeing. And at those privileged moments the table, the child, the grand-parent stand fast and also come toward us in clarity, saying, "Write me."

Thus Claude Vigée is right. It is in meeting the nonbeing with which living particulars are shot through — their mortality, their guilt, their incipient meaninglessness; or in a colony, their wordlessness for us — that we cherish them most fully as what they are. Until that time, we may have cared for them only as things we can own. But in that luminous, perishable aspect they assume their own being for us.

And Abraham Yehoshuah is right. What we know is never a general emptiness — unless we are merely playing with the idea of emptiness, which is a pursuit for dilettantes. We do not encounter Void, we encounter this void and that. And in the concrete ground of their own lapsed existence (which haunts Abraham's own splendid stories, by the way), it is *this* friendship, *this* orange tree, *this* street corner which take on resonance and demand to be written.

Each is home to the other. Hence to give homage to the void for itself is idolatry — but to give homage to the world for itself is idolatry too. To accept nonbeing at home in what is, to accept what is at home in nonbeing, is perhaps the essential act of being human. Certainly it is the beginning of art, and of much philosophy. And (if very great scientists are to be believed) of much of science as well.

And what is — this tree, this enemy, this rooted housing bylaw — makes its mortal being known to us as cadence. That is what I started to hear. In cadence, each thing declares not only *what* it is, nor even *how* it is — but *that* it is. At all. Thus each thing comes to resound in its own silence.

The inauthenticity of our public space is only one such grounding. I am certain that the silence I go into is more than civil. But to write in colonial space is to have that civil silence laid upon you. Whatever else overtakes you, the world you move in and the words you want to use are already cankered with it. When they come alive in cadence, they come alive in it.

★

There is one more thing. The mystique of void is seductive, as I know to my cost. Yet nobody sane will give thanks for what is evil, nor for what keeps scotching vulnerable lovely things without remorse. Death, suffering, deprivation can't just be slotted into some higher scheme of things, as handy aids to ontological contemplation. Evil and innocent pain: to recognize that they teem at the heart of being is not to say that they are comfy, or good, or even acceptable.

That granted, your first response to things that strike at life and goodness undergoes a change, when you discern that everything is most fully itself in the presence of its own emptiness. I cannot say more about that change, however, since I do not understand it very far.

★

A poem enacts in words the presence of what we live among. It arises from the tough, delicate, heartbreaking rooting of what is in its own nonbeing. From that rooting, there arise elemental movements of being: of hunger, of play, of rage, of

24

celebration, of dying. Such movements are always particular, speaking the things which are. A poem enacts those living movements in words.

Quick in its own silence, cadence seeks to issue in the articulate gestures of being.

Roots and Play

Alligator pie, alligator pie,
If I don't get some I think I'm gonna die.
Give away the green grass, give away the sky,
But don't give away my alligator pie . . .

When I started making up nursery rhymes, ten years ago,
I knew what the essence of children's poetry was. This gave
me the confidence to start, and the vision to persevere. And
at this conference on young people's literature, I would love
to share the thing I grasped so clearly then.

I'd love to, but I can't. For the essence of children's poetry
went clean out of my head a year or two later. I lost it the
hard way. I used to read new rhymes with my daughters at
bedtime, and then with their friends, and later their classes at
school. But who can ignore that squirming of small behinds,
and then the patter of little tongues as you plod doggedly
ahead with a poem you know should be a winner, by every
theory on earth it should? Except you're nodding off yourself.
Eventually I had to scrap the essence of children's poetry,
since it was no help in writing poems. And I wound up with
a more promiscuous approach. If something works, it's good;
if it doesn't, it isn't; and you never know which it will be until
you try.

But while I no longer remember what children's poetry
should be, perhaps I could say what it is. "Children's Verse: A
Poet's View." Unfortunately, an arm's-length survey of that

kind is off limits too. When I'm writing, it's as if the whole of children's poetry existed for one purpose: to let me scuffle through it for potent rhythms, tweaks of language, unexpected moves. Random flashpoints for poems of my own. And during this search (which is more like a trance, since I have no idea what I'm looking for), the last thing I'm interested in is breadth or objectivity. I just wolf down what others have done, so I can go and do otherwise. To present myself now as a detached observer would falsify that process.

But if I'm barred from critical overviews, and I can't remember my own theories, what is there left to talk about? There's one thing I could explore. Every so often I find myself pondering the experience of writing, to try and make sense of it. The results don't usually describe my conscious intentions in the past. Nor do they supply a recipe for the future. But they do permit some after-the-fact conversation.

1. *The Birthday Party*

I'm not exactly big,
    And I'm not exactly little,
But being Five is best of all
    Because it's in the middle . . .

In company with most adults, I have a number of children still intact in my nervous system. Like growth rings on a tree. I find I can enjoy a two-year-old's fun, hold my breath at her tribulations, get bored with her silliness — and do so as a fellow two-year-old. I feel a similar resonance with a six-year-old, a ten-year-old, a twelve-year-old. There are a whole series of children inside me, who twig to the world on their own terms. And the key to writing for kids — for me, at least — is to get in touch with one of those children, and go where his instincts lead me. On the other hand, if I start from my adult notion of what a child will enjoy I end up with something condescending, pasted onto the child's life from the outside.

People sometimes ask me what age a poem was written for. And they're surprised when I blink and look trapped. But how would *I* know? Some youngster inside myself was simply enjoying the thing as it happened; I'm curious to see how old he was myself . . . That's how "Alligator Pie" came about. One day in the spring of 1966, I headed out on my bike. As the pedals pumped, I began to hear a mindless refrain — "*al*-li-*ga*-tor *pie* . . . *al*-li-*ga*-tor *pie*" — keeping pace with the circular motion. I tried to ignore it, but the phrase wouldn't leave me alone. Finally I turned around, rode home, and scribbled down the further profundities the rhythm had conjured up. And that was the end of that, or so I thought at the time.

But this is only half the picture. It's true, I want the child to take the lead in the poem. But at the same time, I don't intend to surrender my prerogatives as an adult.

For a start, the thing has to be written well. Whether it wants to be elegant or slapdash, a poem has to clear its own hurdles with grace. It may be simple, but simplicity can be harder to achieve than complexity. And while its way of experiencing things may be a five-year-old's, I can't accept that a poem should play fast and loose with that experience, or recreate it in a merely perfunctory way.

Nor is it just a question of craft. There is a whole rosy-eyed view of childhood which infects the air at times in children's literature. It makes me wonder whether the people who promulgate it have spent more than twenty minutes in the company of flesh-and-blood kids. For myself, I find children the same mixture of good, bad, and indifferent as adults. Some are pretty dull. Others are passionately alive, or winningly gentle or brave. A few are uncommonly grabby, sneaky, or cruel. I don't idealize children en masse any more than I idealize their elders en masse, nor myself en masse.

By the same token, I balk when people eulogize the child's unerring love of good literature. Baloney! My own kids are utterly undiscriminating, as all of us were at their age. They can be transfixed by *Peter Rabbit*, *Where the Wild Things Are*,

Charlotte's Web, Alice in Wonderland. But they can be equally gripped by the tackiest Little Golden Book or Batman comic.

Mind you, there *is* something unique to childhood, particularly the early years. Few young children have learned to inhibit their feelings — at least, not to the extent most grown-ups have. What they feel may be a mixture of nasty and nice, but they feel it directly. The world is still new. And for an adult to reconnect with that nakedness of perception is a kind of grace. But it can be scary, and we may not want the risk. We may just be hoping for an escapist jaunt to a safe and gauzy childhood that never was. I've written poems to skewer that hankering in myself:

> There are midgets at the bottom of my garden.
> Every night they come and play on violins.
> One is named Molly, and one is named Dolly,
> And one has diarrhea, and grins . . .

But the point is not to experience only nice things; it's to experience all things directly again. What I want from a book is that it be a birthday party, to which all our selves are invited. There has to be room for aggressiveness, for terror, for bratty humour. And then I welcome delicate feelings too, and the thrill of a new friend, and those wordless hunches in which we lean into a world that is utterly home:

> Columbine is sweet,
> And sweet alyssum blooming —
> Tell me who you love,
> And I'll whisper what I'm dreaming . . .

★

And if the two do fuse — the child's first-day astonishment, and the adult's more battered wisdom, which can be wise because it has been tested so often, deflowered so many times — if the two do fuse, there can arise a simplicity which occasionally appears on the yonder side of complexity. This

matters. It means that children's literature mediates something we know in the lyrics and songs of maturity as well: a
unification of experience. I came to this first in writing children's verse.

My adult poetry is meditative. It traces the way a person
lives through dissonances and disharmonies, finds the particulars of day-to-day rasping against one another and sometimes
enacting a complex music, which achieves its own concord
without ceasing to express the jangle of the particulars. But
until I started writing children's poetry, I was pretty well
mired in that jangle. I could seldom find a way to release the
lyric sense that also comes, that things are sounding for once
in the same key. Such a unity may be joyous or despairing,
zany or terror-stricken. But for a time it holds, and the
universe comes whole. It's easy to see why falling in love gives
rise to lyric poems, for it lets the world cohere.

This one-ing of the world is the essence of lyricism. What
makes a lyric ring true is not just catchy rhythms or melli-
fluous sounds, but the intuition of a coherence of being. That
makes a single, singing self possible again — or at least glimps-
able — in empathetic response. And lyrical rhythms and
phrasing spring from that intuition; they are its sacramental
embodiment. If they aren't, if they come down to nothing but
technical know-how, they're a trivial form of sacrilege. *The
Secret Garden* and *The Wind in the Willows*, and the best
poems of Milne and de la Mare, are ceremonies of that lyric
coherence. Which means they are as integral to our literature
as the poems of Herrick or Burns.

So my adult poetry could mediate the perception of complexity. But it was in children's poems that the climactic
simplicities emerged, as well as the momentary wholeness
that comes from feeling totally healthy or totally piqued.

Silverly,
  Silverly,
Over the
  Trees

The moon drifts
   By on a
Runaway
   Breeze.

Dozily,
   Dozily,
Deep in her
   Bed,
A little girl
   Dreams with the
Moon in her
   Head.

I don't claim that the lyric is superior to the meditative, nor vice versa. Indeed, I won't be content till I find out how to do them both in the same poem. But it was only when the child and the adult started writing together that I could get near the lyric at all.

2. *Roots*

How far have we come?

I don't write for children; I write *as* children, as an adult children. And I write well only when there is an integration of the two: the child sniffing out the rhythms and notions that excite him, the adult supplying the pacing, the verbal tact that will let them come into their own as poems. And in the directness and wholeness that sometimes prevail, I find a lyric voice that has mostly eluded me in adult work.

What quickens your imagination when you start to write this way? I know two things that have kindled me: roots, and play.

★

There is a shock of recognition that lies in wait in books, which readers in English Canada have discovered mainly in the last few decades. It's so basic, many of you will find it remarkable we took so long to get here. All I can say is, we find it remarkable too.

It is the discovery that excellent writing is rooted in its own time and place — *and these can be your own.* The realization doesn't come in such heady terms, of course. It arises when you read a compelling book by a contemporary and find it speaking *your* place, *your* time, *your* way of being — catching the inflections of how they are more truly than you ever thought possible. Suddenly the book is alive inside your life: very daring, very inevitable, very much just there, like a new intimacy you didn't know about till it happened, but already you're at home with it.

The effect is startling. "Oh," you say, "so that's what it was about! But this is who we *are* . . . You mean, it's okay to be who you are? Literature can be that?"

This confirmation of what is, I call "roots." The kind of book I'm talking about is rooted in its locale, of course. But the book in turn *affords* roots to the reader. Which means, it makes the textures of his everyday life palpable, raises them to imaginative visibility. It's a kind of second nesting.

If you've read for years without discovering this dimension of reading, it comes as a shock, a mild giddiness to find you can have everything you used to have, and roots as well. And *Oedipus Rex* and "Ode to a Nightingale" are not diminished by that. Far from it; you glimpse how they spoke with this extra, primal resonance to the men and women they first rooted. Which is an enrichment of what you already knew in them: the universality their locality springs loose. Yet that local rootedness of a work is its gift to its own time and place, and we can participate in it fully and unself-consciously only with the art of *our* time and place. I would say, as a Canadian wasp, that it is Margaret Laurence, Alice Munro, and Al Purdy who have bestowed that gift of roots most fully on people like me.

★

Fog Lifting

In Stewiacke and Mushaboom
I didn't see a thing;
At Musquodoboit Harbour, I could
Hear the foghorn sing;

At Ecum Secum I discovered
Colours in the sea —
And I learned to look at living things
In Shubenacadie.

About 1965, as I was beginning to read Mother Goose to my first daughter, these things were tumbling around in my head. And I found myself starting to chafe. In one way, my thoughts seemed ludicrous, not worth taking seriously. But in another, I had no choice.

What I was thinking was this. "Here is a little girl, not yet two, and she's getting bounced to the rhythm of curds and whey, of pipers and pence, of piglets and plum pudding and pease porridge hot — and she hasn't the foggiest idea what they are. For shame! Thought control! Mother Goose is an imperialist conspiracy!"

But that seemed pretty silly — if only because, had she been getting bounced to the rhythm of fire hydrants and T-4 slips and dominion-provincial conferences, she wouldn't have known what they were either. And I didn't want to deprive her of Mother Goose. Was the argument taking me in a doctrinaire, book-banning direction? I hoped not.

"Still," I went on, "isn't it bizarre that before she's two this child should learn what Canadians know by heart — that the imagination always leads to the city of elsewhere? That we enter it as barbarians from beyond the gates? Do I really want to teach her that?"

Well, I thought, that's not entirely true either. Mother Goose *is* about our lives. About sounds and rhythms chasing themselves in and out; about the destiny on earth we share with people in centuries past.

But while I agreed with this, and still do, I couldn't escape the sense that you are the poorer if you never find your own time and place speaking words of their own. Finally, I arrived at a discovery which struck me with the full force of the banality it possesses, and yet felt momentous and almost illicit, since I had never heard it said out loud.

The nursery rhymes I love, and my children love, are exotic to us. (I still don't know what a tuffet is, and in a perverse way I hope I never find out.) But they were in no way exotic to the people who first chanted them. "Three little pigs went to market": that once had the everyday immediacy of — of what? "Three wiener dogs went to Loblaws," something like that. The air of far-off charm and simpler pastoral existence which now hangs over Mother Goose was in no way part of those rhymes' initial delight. I don't want to wish away that aura; it is part of their having endured in time. But the people who told those rhymes for centuries would be boggled if they could experience them as children do now — as a collection of references to things they've never seen, places they've never been to, in words they will often meet only in those verses. The rhymes themselves haven't changed. But where they once confirmed their listeners' roots, articulated "home" in the earliest season of their lives, they no longer do. To claim that gift today, I realized, we have to look elsewhere. In our own backyard.

So I started to listen for poems in the hockey sticks and high-rise my children knew. I wasn't sure how to begin, but I mooched around.

The readiest thing was to play with the place names that dot the country. I remember my excitement when I came across a poem by the New Zealander, Denis Glover. He was coaxing his home to sing in a way my body could feel:

In Plimmerton, in Plimmerton,
The little penguins play,
And one dead albatross was found
At Karehana Bay . . .

35

In this country, the native names in particular have a gorgeous incantatory lilt. Here's a rhyme that simply hunkers down into their music:

> If I lived in Temagami,
> Temiskaming, Kenagami,
> Or Lynx, or Michipicoten Sound,
> I wouldn't stir the whole year round
>
> Unless I went to spend the day
> At Bawk, or Nottawasaga Bay,
> Or Missinabi, Moosonee,
> Or Kahshe or Chicoutimi.

And here's a bouncing song that ventures further afield:

> Who shall be king of the little kids' swing?
> Jimmy's the king of the little kids' swing,
> *With a bump on your thumb*
> *And a thump on your bum*
> *And tickle my tum in Toronto . . .*

Mind you, a lot of the things I tried in the map-reading mode were pretty pedestrian; they had nothing going for them but the purity of their programmatic intent, and I threw them out. Gradually I realized that the externals didn't have to be so self-conscious. If it felt right to include something explicitly Canadian, fine. If it didn't feel right, equally fine. There was a mounting sense of excitement as I abandoned the more crusading aspects of the thing, and discovered there really was a music in the lives of the children I know and am. There was no need to *give* a poem roots; if you just sat still for a spell, letting things find their way into you, they would be happy to come as themselves, and sometimes be poems. It gave me a sense of almost physical release as places, things, experiences, even individual words, which as far as I knew had never been set vibrating in poems, found their way into these verses.

Skyscraper, skyscraper,
Scrape me some sky:
Tickle the sun
While the stars go by.

Tickle the stars
While the sun's climbing high,
Then skyscraper, skyscraper
Scrape me some sky.

I remember especially the fall of 1973, sitting all day in the
basement of a house in downtown Toronto, hearing the trains
racket along the tracks across the street, and waiting on a
whole clutch of these poems that installed themselves on the
page in a space of six weeks. And about 5:30 every afternoon
I'd charge upstairs, waving some new piece of paper, and we'd
celebrate and sometimes tinker the thing. And old poems got
revised with a flourish, for the umpteenth time, and it was all
a bit of a high. Not that those pieces were lofty philosophical
excursions; as time went by they seemed to get more light-
hearted, light-footed, light-headed. But since I usually work
like a mole, groping my way through incessant drafts, I don't
think I'll ever forget that time.

*

One poem from that little run shows how far the business of
roots had come. I'd grown fascinated with a love affair my son
was carrying on. But to coax it into words would be tricky,
since he was only two. The challenge had nothing to do with
contemporary references (apart from day care), and everything to do with enacting the inflections of a child's inner life.
Catching those textures could afford a subtler, more inward
kind of rooting.

I've got a Special Person
   At my day care, where I'm in.
Her name is Mrs. Something
   But we mostly call her Lynn.

'Cause Lynn's the one that shows you
    How to Squish a paper cup.
And Lynn's the one that smells good
    When you make her pick you up.
    (She smells good when she picks you up.)

She knows a lot of stories
    And she reads them off by heart.
There's one about a Bear, but I
    Forget the other part.

She bit me on my knee once, 'cause I
    Said she couldn't scream,
And then I sent her in the hall,
    And then we had Ice Cream.

I guess I'm going to marry Lynn
    When I get three or four,
And Lynn can have my Crib, or else
    She'll maybe sleep next door,

'Cause Jamie wants to marry Lynn
    And live here too, he said.
(I guess he'll have to come, but he's
    Too Little for a Bed.)

By this point, the quest for roots had virtually dissolved as a conscious pursuit. If a poem could utter its locale by its inflections as much as its content, the search did not depend primarily on capturing the externals of time and place. It depended on writing in a way that rang true.

I had come full circle. When I was twenty, I wanted to write well, and I never thought about roots. Fifteen years later, I still want to write well. But while I've been much preoccupied with roots in the meantime, I've stopped pressing to wedge them into poems. Yet that continuity is only apparent, for by now the quest has passed into the reflexes of the writing itself.

3. *Play*

WAL — *I had a* DOG,
    And his name was Doogie,
    And I don't know why
    But he liked to boogie;

    He boogied all night
    He boogied all day
    He boogied in a rude
    Rambunctious way . . .

Coming out of a WASP tradition, I began to realize in my twenties that I was emotionally constricted. There were feelings I didn't seem to have access to, although I could sense their pent-up power. Or if I did connect with them, I couldn't express them in daily life. Or if they came out there, I still couldn't enact them in poems. What I craved was the chance to *play* — to unleash this buried life in a kind of rehearsal and wooing.

And that too led me to write as an adult children. For the task of children is to play, and thereby rehearse the lives they will later live. Their play may be trivial or profound, celebratory or cruel; in fact, such breadth is a characteristic of play. It ranges from the simple release of energy to rituals of loss and celebration, enacting a gamut of possible selves in the safe house of let's-pretend. As Huizinga says in *Homo Ludens*, "Frivolity and ecstasy are the twin poles between which play moves."

So my children's work unfurled new gestures of being human. "New," not in the sense that no one had ever used this emotional musculature before. But new in the sense of breaking taboos: against goofiness, anger, rejoicing, bodily grace — whatever energies had been tamped down by my culture. Enacting those impulses on the page *was* the play I am speaking of.

Mind you, it made me self-conscious at first. I was still trying to find my place as an adult poet. And how readily would the unfamiliar music of *Civil Elegies* be heard, I wondered, if I popped up at the same time with meter and rhyme and verses for two-year-olds? But the impulse to play was too strong for my career anxieties.

Let me start with the poems I wrote for older children. Many, I see now, approached the challenge of play as their undeclared theme. Often they brought some conventional character into collision with a vibrant, larger-than-life personage. The effect was to raise the question, "What are you going to do about *this*? Can you handle it?" And the response was different each time, since I had no fixed answer.

Here's one stanza from the earliest of these pieces, "The Cyclone Visitors":

Rasputin the Monk
Is dancing, dead drunk,
   On the top of the New City Hall.
I've called for a cop.
I've begged him to stop,
   But he will not stop dancing at all —
The gall!
   If he doesn't stop dancing, he'll fall.
You can't *dance* on a New City Hall!

There are three vignettes in the poem, and they all explore the same possibility — that the bawdy, the holy, the untameably vital might remain off limits for keeps. The purse-lipped speaker is clearly not taking any chances with zanies like this. And that's where I started, imagining the worst.

There are a variety of such encounters in *Nicholas Knock and Other People*. Mr. Hoobody exudes a gross, subversive energy, which tantalizes the child who meets him. Ookpik is a blur of pure lyric grace — and this time the voice of the poem follows suit: "Like a snail in a trance, like a flare, / Like an acrobat turning to air." You can find more variations in "The Thing," "Wellington the Skeleton," or (my own favourite) "The Cat and the Wizard."

40

"Nicholas Knock" approached the motif more consciously than the rest. By the time I wrote it, I could recognize the shape my imagination kept coming out with. Here the emissary of larger life is the silver honkabeest, whose intermittent presence haunts Nicholas:

> *Frisky, most silver, serene —*
> *bright step at the margins of air, you*
> *tiny colossus and*
> *winsome and*
> *master me, easy in sunlight, you*
> *gracious one come to me, live in*
> *my life.*

★

That's one way of approaching the challenge of play: by embodying the taboo energies in some vital character, and imagining what would happen if you met up with him. And it's a relatively straightforward matter to track the changes the poetry rings on this motif. There's a comfortable fit between this approach and critical categories we already have at hand.

But the poems for younger children take a different tack. They're not about the challenge of play; they simply *play*. Often that's all they do. And they play at such an elemental level that it is a good deal harder to articulate what's going on.

How do you discuss sheer play in poetry? I don't know any widely accepted approach. In fact, I'm not sure we have a language for talking about it at all. In trying to pin down this quality, people often call it "nonsense." But I believe that term is better reserved for something different: for work which weaves together logic and irrationality, and in the process demolishes many of our assumptions about the way things are. In this specialized sense of the term, Lewis Carroll is the master of nonsense.

> He thought he saw an Elephant
>   That practised on a fife:

> He looked again, and found it was
>   A letter from his wife.
> "At length I realise," he said,
>   "The bitterness of Life!" . . .
>
> He thought he saw an Argument
>   That proved he was the Pope:
> He looked again, and found it was
>   A Bar of Mottled Soap.
> "A fact so dread," he faintly said,
>   "Extinguishes all hope!"

Now, that is true nonsense: an elegantly impotent rehearsal of logic in a universe where logic fails to apply. And I would be honoured to write in that company. But the fact is, it's not my primary bent. What people speak of as nonsense in my work is something else.

I want to call it "play." But if I resort to the word again, I need to distinguish what I mean from the previous usage. "Children's play" takes in the whole gamut of let's-pretend: strutting about as the king of the castle, burying a deceased insect, caring for dolls, shooting somebody dead. We've already considered that broad sense of the term. But now I want to apply it to a narrower band of the spectrum — to high spirits, kibitzing, the release of animal energy that we recognize as "playful." And what I want to know is this: when a poem plays in this sense, what does its play consist of?

When I ponder that question, it leads me straight to Mother Goose.

*

The thing that boggles me in nursery rhymes is how they rely on the absolute basics: raw sound and rhythm, directed by movements of feeling. That's as close to pure music as poetry can get. And for the poet, it means there's no place to hide. Not images; not stories; not bright ideas. Either the thing works at this primal level, or it doesn't work at all.

Consider a consummate eleven-word poem:

> Jack be nimble,
> Jack be quick,
> Jack jump over
> The candlestick.

I don't know how many times I've sat and repeated that rhyme, trying to figure out what makes it work. You'll follow where we're going most readily if you try it for yourself. Say the verse several times; slow it down to half speed; exaggerate the inflections. You'll feel it take on the force of a chant or incantation . . .

Now, try changing a few of the words, without altering the meaning. Put in words with different sounds:

> Jack be speedy,
> Jack be quick,
> Jack hop over
> The candlestick.

Put in words that change the rhythm:

> Jack be nimble,
> Jack be quick,
> Jack hurdle over
> The candlestick.

Can you feel the way the little mantra goes askew, stops enacting its own dynamic with such absolute poise? When the verbal play doesn't work, we can sense it in our muscles, our breathing. And if you go back to the original version, you'll feel even more clearly how right it is. But what *makes* it right?

Whatever it may be, it's nothing that scholarship can reveal. Iona and Peter Opie tell us the rhyme probably derives from the game of candle leaping, which was practised for centuries in England. You put a lighted candle on the floor, and tried to

jump over it without extinguishing the flame; if you succeeded, you had good luck for a year. But while that provides
some engaging background, it gets us no closer to understanding the poem's play.

Since I mess around with words, my inclination is to look
for the explanation somewhere else. Namely, in the soundscape of the poem: the kinetic shape which the sounds and
stresses create. But the point is not just to show that such a
shape exists. Read any four lines from the telephone book,
and you'll hear a pattern of one kind or another in the sounds.
So what? The question is, what does the pattern accomplish?
What story is being told in the auditory and kinaesthetic
dimension of the poem?

Translating that music into words can take a disproportion-
ate, almost risible amount of space. But that comes with the
territory. We understand these things by body knowledge first.
And when we translate it into head knowledge, we're displac-
ing it from its native habitat. Please bear with the drawn-out
process of translation in what follows.

"Jack Be Nimble" is about a game. Even if we've never heard
of candle leaping, it's clear that Jack is being urged to show
his mettle with a mighty jump. That is: the *subject* of the poem
is play.

But while "play" is a key term in our discussion, it doesn't help
to pin that label on the content. Not because it doesn't apply,
but because the content is not what makes the words skip and
soar in the first place. We saw that when we substituted
"speedy" for "nimble," "hurdle" for "jump." The content was
still "play" — but the poem no longer *played*. Or not with the
same grace and verve.

Let's try again.

Not only is "Jack Be Nimble" about a game. It acts out the
stages *in* the game. The poem is a starter's command, which
follows the general form: "On your mark — get set — GO!" It
could have read, "Be nimble — be quick — JUMP!" The poem
gives us Jack's preparatory tensing, in lines one and two; and
then, stretching across lines three and four, the jump itself.

With that in mind, consider the poem as a tissue of sound. You'll notice there are two stressed syllables in each line. The first line, for instance, goes, "*Jack* be / *nim*-ble." And if you listen to the vowels you've stressed, you'll hear, "*a . . . ih*" (in "*Jack*" and "*nim-*").

Now, follow the shape which the stressed syllables create. They run:

a . . . ih	(*Jack . . . nim-*)
a . . . ih	(*Jack . . . quick*)
a . . . oh	(*Jack . . . o-*)
a . . . ih	(*can- . . . -stick*)

But this is striking. The poem departs from the basic pattern ("*a . . . ih*") only once — just as Jack is achieving liftoff ("*a . . . oh*"). And it returns to the basic pattern as he returns to the floor. In a way that's almost too subtle to articulate, the music of the poem is acting out its own content; the action unfolds right in the sound of the words. (Which is why "Jack be speedy" was such a dud; it sabotaged the sound pattern before it began.)

Are we aware of this when we read the rhyme? I never was, though I *felt* it clearly enough. Did whoever wrote "Jack Be Nimble" set out to create this effect? I have no way of knowing, but I bet they didn't. I bet they lucked into it, by hunch and inspiration. At most, I bet they kept on playing with the words until they felt right — meaning, until the sound gave the kind of subliminal satisfaction we've teased into daylight. Perhaps it happened as the rhyme was reshaped over generations, till it stabilized in this form.

However it came about, the result is a verse we can't get out of our heads, our bodies even. And the reason for that is the rococo aplomb of the soundscape, which is both shapely in itself, and a live enactment of the poem's meaning.

★

Something parallel is true of the rhythm. Listen to the verse again — this time, treating it as a tissue of lighter and stronger stresses.

The basic rhythmic unit is familiar: a strong beat followed by a weak. A trochee, for those who observe metrical terminology. And each line consists of two trochees. The first line sets up the pattern unmistakably: "*Jack* be / *nim*-ble." The second line does what an English-speaker's ear expects — it drops the final weak syllable, leaving us to hear it as a rest: "*Jack* be / *quick*."

But notice what happens next. There are two departures from the rhythmic pattern. The third line begins with two strong beats: "*Jack jump*." Pronouncing these two heavy stresses slows the line down — perhaps to the extent of a tiny pause between "Jack" and "jump," as our tongue makes its way through the viscous consonants. (I also hear a lengthening of the "J" in "Jack," though I wouldn't press the point.) All this reconfigures the dynamics of the poem in a subtle but unmistakable way. And it's not gratuitous that this slower, more thudding rhythm occurs where it does. This is where Jack is getting set, digging in for the leap. (Which is why "hurdle" didn't work; it made the rhythm contradict that movement.)

The other departure comes in the final line. There's an extra weak syllable at the beginning — the word "the." It's a grace note, which gives the rhythm an added skip . . . You can finish the case yourself. The extra syllable lengthens the duration of the leap, mimes Jack's time in the air. And when the first strong stress of the line explodes on "*can-*" — which we're likely to say with the strongest stress and the highest pitch of any syllable in the poem — we feel an adrenalin boost, as Jack soars over the flame.

On its tiny scale, "Jack Be Nimble" works beautifully. It takes an absurd number of words to describe what transpires in the soundscape. But in our bodies, we register its shape at once. The shape of a leap; the shape of a *yes!* of triumph. And if we want to enter the poem's play, it is to this dimension we must attend.

Do all nursery rhymes enact their content the way "Jack Be Nimble" does? Not in precise detail. Or at least, I doubt they do. But I haven't sat down to analyze very many. I'm content to absorb their play with my body — experience it directly, play along. What I *am* certain of is that every nursery rhyme we lug around with us still, imprinted in memory at the cellular level, is unforgettable precisely because its play unfolds with shapely panache in this aural/kinaesthetic dimension.

★

Where does that get us?

A good nursery rhyme is an *incantation*. The sheer sound and rhythm enact a spell of some kind: one that meshes both with the way the muscles of the body want to move, and with some primitive intuition of how the world fits together and flows.

This helps explain a striking feature of nursery rhymes. Consider how many start with a line of pure sound, virtually uncontaminated by meaning:

Hickory, dickory, dock . . .

Handy spandy, Jack-a-Dandy . . .

Peter, Peter, pumpkin eater . . .

It's a magic spell, ushering us into a parallel world of the imagination. Only after the spell has been cast do the sounds distil into sense. Then the play of incantation can proceed.

Or that is my hunch. But you can't verify it by looking at a nursery rhyme on the page, because it will simply look back at you. That's like trying to enjoy a piece of music by reading the score. You have to have a very young child on your knee. And you have to do the poem with her — very slowly, with a certain gleeful passion. Let each syllable happen like a new day in your life. Then a rhyme comes something like a birthday, and a quickening in the rhythm like a new season.

These similes are not idle, though they do no more than point to what I mean. It really is possible with a good nursery rhyme — "Jack Be Nimble," for instance — to experience the incantation this way. Rhythm in the words, translated via the jounce of your knee to the child's bum, and then up her spine. Sounds that open out like parasols, a succession of colours, almost meaning something but mainly filling your mutual field of attention one after the other, and sometimes sliding back on themselves when the same sound rhymes. Because the medium of nursery rhymes is oral and communal, you encounter these constituents as an environment. One which triggers the old rhythms of cyclical delight: stability, and the excursions of novelty. And you can feel those instincts stirring inside you, if you help the child give you permission.

This may sound like mystification. It isn't. I experience it all the time in nursery rhymes, though I don't take the words I've used to describe it as gospel. Nor do I know *how* you find rhythms and sounds that cast a spell, enact an incantation. All I do is play around with words until they work.

And that leaves me with renewed admiration for the anonymous masters of Mother Goose. Because what looks terribly simple, simpleminded even — to plunk down a bunch of words and notions, and make children skip and laugh to them — is a great deal harder than it seems. It's undeniable that some rhymes sink into their imaginations, their bodies almost, like water into a sponge. While others remain clever, inert little exercises which never come home to a single child. But there's seldom an obvious explanation why it's one or the other; either you get it right, or the poem goes belly up.

When you set out to play directly in words, you're like a jazz musician during improvisation. There's no safety net.

*

How much are these ruminations worth?

It may be of interest to know that one children's poet was propelled by a craving for roots and a need to play. But once you sit down to read a poem, that falls away. The only thing that matters is whether it lives and breathes; understanding what prompted its gestation has nothing to do with finding that you enjoy it directly. Or not.

Nor does it give me any clue about what to write next. I'm pleased with these poems, but like most writers I revolve around the things I haven't written yet; they're my centre of gravity. And when I look back at the books from that obscure perspective, I'm anything but satisfied.

Not so much because of what's in them, but because of what isn't. I spent so much energy just clearing a way toward rooted play, and so little time making its poems. And I think: there are terrors, and joys, and states of daily despair and amazement that I was barely making a pass at here. How could I take this as anything but a first flirtation — trying to pass off mischievousness as bawdy vitality, and a timid sense of discomfort as holy terror?

Then I read the poems with children and grown-ups again, and they do trigger the things I was reaching for, and I no longer know what to think. Finally I let them go, and turn back to the poems still buzzing to be written. They are what compels me, though I know that once they're safe in words they too will slide away, leaving me confused, exultant, still in wait for the cranky miracle.

Polyphony

Enacting a Meditation

It is time to speak more carefully of cadence, and the way it shapes a meditation. But it's hard to see where to begin — both because everything depends on everything else, and because cadence itself is the source of speech about cadence.

Bear with this beginning. It is spare, compressed, even somewhat airless. But it's not meant as a series of definitions handed down from the podium. It's an attempt — slightly over-determined, I'm afraid — to concentrate on the nuclear hunches from which the subject radiates. And to keep from domesticating them with categories which would distort them with a premature clarity.

1.

A meditative poem exists because something has wooed it to be.

The poem woos that something in return, seeking to mime its gestures of being.

The something is cadence.

*

It is all but impossible to speak nakedly of cadence. What you can hope to do is uncover the way a poem participates in its life.

2.

The medium in which poetry exists is *voice*.

The voice of a poem embodies a given timbre of being. It mediates one of the wavelengths on which things are.

To hear a poem's voice is to enter its embodiment of the world.

★

Specific vocal inflections are created by technical elements. By line lengths; line breaks; syntax; rhythms; levels of diction; sound colour; interweaving of imagery, irony, statement . . .

But technique is not our concern here. The nature of voice, as the medium of poetry, is.

3.

Most poems are monophonic; they're written in a single voice.

★

The most common single voice in contemporary poetry is the one which *states*. "I think of how you betrayed me, and I feel angry."

What does that voice embody? A discursive equanimity, which reports on its feelings (and everything else) with arm's-length detachment. But the feelings themselves have no incarnate reality in the poem. They never dislodge the declarative tone, never achieve embodiment on their own.

The poem no more "feels angry" than it feels pink. The voice gives the lie to its own utterance.

★

(If the poem wants to ring true, let it canvass the details of the betrayal — and let it canvass them *angrily*.

Anger need not be mentioned by name. But it must be embodied in the movement & texture & pitch of the recollection.

This calls for passionate vocal tact. As do inflections of coltishness, ecstasy, musing, despair. As does any authentic inflection.)

★

The discursive voice embodies one valid human strain, of editorializing urbanity. But if that's the only voice we hear, it excludes all other currents in the speaker's makeup.

And it's not just the speaker's nature that gets straitened. Other people and wars and trees and daily multifarious events all go de-selved, within a vocal range which cannot embody their indigenous tonalities. The whole world is shrunk to a single, reportorial wavelength.

4.

The voice which states — clipped, descriptive, distanced from what it observes — is the dominant monotone in contemporary poetry. It reigns in *New Yorker* poems, and in most British verse.

As the vehicle for one narrow range of being human, this is a decorous voice. Anything deeper, more epochally alive, it minifies.

★

A monophonic poem which embodies a different voice than the discursive — *any* different voice — is already a signal achievement.

5.

But what makes a poem univocal is not its specific voice. It's the fact that one voice is prolonged throughout the poem.

Such monophony is not intrinsically a bad thing. A short poem might fly apart if a second voice came in at line six. The poem may need to be in a single tone.

But single-voiced poetry — whether discursive, dithyrambic,

or in any other univocal timbre — is not my subject. I speak of it only in order to go beyond it.

6.

Most readers can read monophonically. Most poets oblige.

But a poem can change the inflection of its voice five times in thirty lines. It can rage, state, noodle, cavort, then shudder with grief.

Polyphony in writing is the art of orchestrating successive voices across a work.

7.

"Polyphony." Many sounds: many voices.

Polyphonic music traces out two or more melodic lines at the same time, using several instruments, or several human voices.

Polyphonic poetry is different. It moves from one tonality to another, and on through consecutive voices.

8.

The shift from inflection to inflection, the clash and resonance of timbres, traces out a trajectory of meditation.

★

That is: an authentic meditation must *enact*.

It does so by living its way from one inflection to the next.

For it to be a meditation at all, a poem must embody in voice the way its experience of the world is initially focused — and then proceed to envoice *another* focusing; and then *another*. To live its way to deeper and more complete knowing, which is what a meditation does, it must move from one vocal embodiment to another.

The plot of a meditation is enacted by these shifting inflections.

Otherwise it hasn't budged an inch. No matter how much the content may change, it is still colonized within a single voice: that of a thesis, a lament, a tirade.

9.

To write polyphonically is to contest poetry as it is now written. Perhaps to repudiate it altogether. To walk off that field, and try to find the real one.

10.

Just a minute, Mr. Lee. What have you got against a voice of calm statement? Or against orderly thinking?

Nothing at all. My point was different.

We meditate with our whole lives: with our passions and mind and flesh and our past and our deepest hungers. So in a meditation, the act of *stating* — stating an idea, a feeling, whatever — has to arise, if it's going to arise, as exactly that. As one action in the overall process. It is no more normative than any other gesture: snarling, stroking a memory, kicking up its heels. And it has to belong where it occurs; it has to well up precisely when it does because the meditating consciousness is propelled to state the idea — *this* idea, at *this* point — by the complex pressure of all that has come before. What's more, the idea has to find its proper voice in the flow. One time it may be shaggy and impassioned; again, dry and precise; another time it might be goofy.

That is, the act of stating must be vocally embodied — *as* an action. And play a decorous part within the larger orchestration. Not just emerge as a string of propositions, which are made to stand as the whole poem.

None of these reservations makes it improper to state, reflect, declare. But only if you do so as a full and variegated human being, who is meditating upon a complex world with everything he is. Grieving and raging and celebrating and thinking and remembering — they all have to be orchestrated.

Hmmm. Perhaps.

11.

Sometimes one inflection will hold for twenty lines; at other times there may be three changes in two lines. With voices flickering or criss-cross or interlaced. Till there are scores and scores of tonalities across the piece, kinetic, and the whole thing starts to sing across inside itself. Voice over voice — that harmony. And what the orchestration of voices begins to enact is the fullness of cadence.

That's part of what I mean. It's a start. It still isn't right.

12.

So far, we haven't considered the content of meditation. In one way, the subject is irrelevant to polyphony. But in another way it isn't, for the meditating voice can scarcely proceed without meditating *on* something. There is hardly ever such a thing as content-free voice.

But that way of putting it is dubious. It's not just that the "voice" of a poem has a certain "content." In fact, there are three things involved: a meditating consciousness; the content of its meditation; and the voice in which they're embodied.

13.

In one aspect, polyphony must be heard as the inflected trajectory of the poem's content, held in the meditating consciousness.

That is: abstracting to an "objective" pole, a meditation consists of a series of thematic movements. Each is a new stage in an argument. And the content must reconfigure the voice at every stage.

★

In another aspect, polyphony must be heard as the inflected trajectory of the poem's consciousness, attending to the content.

That is: abstracting to a "subjective" pole, a meditation consists of a series of psychic movements. Each is a new stage in a quest. And the stance of consciousness must reconfigure the voice at every stage.

*

Both abstractions are useful. Neither is more than an abstraction.

The originating unity, which is schematized in both, is the kinesis of polyphony itself: the vocal trajectory which the meditation enacts. In a mature meditation, content and consciousness are both embodied in the voice, hence coextensive and seamless. If their polyphony rings true, we can divide them only after the fact.

14.

To read a meditation rightly is a matter of hearing its longer vocal rhythms. The way you hear successive movements in a symphony: absorbing local passages, and simultaneously discerning the larger progression from one to the next.

This vocal trajectory, which moves (and leaps, and ricochets) from one focus of content/consciousness to the next, furnishes the basic formal language of a meditation.

15.

Such a trajectory doesn't just follow a fixed itinerary, like checking in at pre-established points on a route map.

The poem has to live its way through a course of attending, and be changed by what it discovers at each stage. That change might carry it anywhere.

The guide is what rings true in the voice.

*

So it's not as if you had a battery of portable styles, which you slather over whatever new content or mood comes along. The voice gets generated — often for the first and only time — by the torque and drift and tensions of each new place you move to. You may spend days or weeks, months even, finding how to utter the five-line place you've entered.

Finding what that new place *is* — which comes to the same thing. You first occupy it when you hit the voice that rings true for *this* moment of consciousness, focused by *this* burden of content.

16.

To follow the grain of a meditation, you need to listen to the music of the space it's enacting — the musics, really, because it pounds *and* loops *and* shimmies *and* tumbles. I wish I could do them all at once.

The "movements" are a series of improvised recoils. Like body English out loud. They may come in off-key with the one before, and the one before that, but you realize they've got their own right pitch themselves. And then you hear them getting changed by one another, and a funny concord starts to orchestrate itself out of the clash and changes.

★

Say it's ticking along very quietly, just ticking over, and then all of a sudden it spurts straight up for a bit — ka-*ching!* — till you realize there's a long slow roll coming in from the far side now, it crests right across the spurt and carries the thing out the other side for 20 lines maybe, with just a bit of a tremolo around the edges. Bit of lace. Whatever.

17.

Very pretty. Very poetic. But there's one thing I don't understand. When I read a description of an "open" poem, I can't see why anything has to occur exactly where it does. Or even, sometimes, why it has to be in the poem at all. What governs all these random leapings-about that you've described?

Hunches. Trial and error. Hearing the music in your forearms, and trying not to muff it. God knows you spend enough time muffing it, exploring dead-ends you have to abandon.

But that doesn't tell us anything. If you start with no pre-established plan, and content and form are both up for grabs, and you're just winging it, how can you tell when you've muffed it and when you haven't?

What happened to the ideal of organic form? How can you do anything but set down bits and pieces and link them up arbitrarily? What does formal coherence even consist of, in this kind of poem?

There's something deeper, but I can't get at it yet. Something is enforced on you. See, I know my stuff moves around a lot. But I try to . . .

It's true. There's nothing in what I've said that accounts for the emergence of organic form. Nor even for the practical leads you get — since with or without a formal theory, you do discover a way ahead.

I haven't said a thing about the source of coherence in polyphonic writing.

18.

What needs more room to breathe is the way cadence impinges on you when you're writing.

★

It begins long before individual words come clear: that's one thing. Before they are any kind of guide to what's getting born.

And cadence *teems*. As a kind of magnetic din, a silent raucous multiform atmospheric tumult you move around in, very clean though. And always: when you perceive it, when you don't. I could write hymns to it, almost. Not to the poems, to what I hear.

What *is* it?

It's there, that's all. It's *here*. Not just to sponsor poems . . . And I know: if you could somehow screen out the literal meaning of words in the final poem, their polyphony would still enact the gestures of cadence. That dance of voices.

Of course you can't separate the play of vocal inflections from the literal meaning of words. But the music does exist at a pre-signifying level. And hearing it recapitulates the way the spurt and shimmy and hover and lunge first came at you — which was, they came tumbling through you long before there were words to flesh them out. You were galvanized by cadence, not yet knowing what its shape was. Let alone its content.

And what you need, miming that summons, is an utterly supple medium: a voice that can metamorphose endlessly from inflection to inflection. Under the press of the necessities of the cadence it's born in. And borne in. Gradually at times; or abruptly, but with no sense of the gears being ground. Nor of it being stage-managed in its changes. Like a field of luminous force, knotted and folding and stalling and skittering back, perpetual live energy. But not rarified, not removed, it's not ideal; this worries me almost — does it mean worshipping whatever is, good and evil like goulash? Because always it's just there, thudding like somebody breathing, magisterial, right now we're in it . . . Oink . . . Selah . . .

What *is* it?

19.

See, I *know* my stuff moves around. But I go in the straightest line I can. I hate obscurity, I hate gussied-up decoration. There's just the one clean trajectory of attending; you hew to the grain. But in the space of cadence, what people see as straight lines — standard logical associations, received emotional, literary, even tonal ones — may bear no relation to the actual currents of that space. So if you move in a conventional straight line, you falsify the grain of how things go about being themselves. Which means, you falsify the grain of the texture of the necessities they're thrown in, and configured by.

20.

What moves around is voice. Content-in-consciousness, embodied in voice.

21.

It's like the way — to use a limited analogy — it's like the way "straight" lines on the surface of the earth are actually curved. They don't exist in a flat plane to begin with. Suppose you took a straight line from Toronto to Barcelona: you'd tunnel through millions of tons of the planet, you wouldn't be following the curve of the surface you live on. But that curvature determines what the shortest distance between two points *is*, on the surface of earth.

And moving with the curvature of earth is what we do every time we take a step. Going in a straight line is an imaginary activity for us. We don't exist in two dimensions; we were confused for far too long, we thought we lived in Euclid's mind.

22.

The grain of cadential space is no more straight than that of our motion on the earth.

But cadential space curves more unpredictably than earth's does — and more than that, it eddies and throbs and hiccups and tumbles and loops. It's not just a matter of recognizing that natural lines of motion curve regularly in three dimensions, rather than extending in two. The space of cadence keeps changing its local texture, with all sorts of unexpected mutations.

So the ground rules of straightness, of direct utterance, change too.

For a spell, cadential space may extend monophonically — as though in two dimensions. Then curve off into three. Then it may abruptly pucker, bunch, recoil, explode, go becalmed. You have to feel out the changing texture as you go.

It's odd to speak of "feeling it out," when the poem still doesn't exist. There's nothing you can point to and say, "*This* is what's guiding me." But the energy is there; you sense it intuitively, and you put yourself at its behest.

23.

I speak of a "space" of cadence, and that may imply that a poem is a static map which describes it. But it's not like that at all. A meditation is the *act* of moving through textured space. It's wholly kinetic. And the words on the page are the track of its going.

A meditation doesn't describe a space; it enacts one. It is a finding-the-grain-of-cadential-space, and a letting-it-breathe-in-voice.

24.

And it's cadence that guides you. A meditation must sense its gestures, and woo them and mime them.

So you suss out how the grain of the energy flows in each new piece you start. And you let the poem flow with it, till the voice gets inflected by every whorl and spurt and flicker along the way.

And you can feel the heft of the cells in your arms, your neck, your sexual centre — you feel your hopes and forebears straining to reach those articulate gestures of being. You can't compel them. But once you find the flow, once you enter the jostle and hover and rush of the right full carnal gesture in words there is such a de-kinking, such a deep sense of release into what is quick and still and implacably there, that it nourishes you utterly. And for a time, at least, you don't understand what other calling makes sense.

25.

It's a paradox.

In such a cosmos, polyphony is the craft of direct utterance. What is more complex is simpler. Because a shifting tonality lets you hew to the grain, enact the rich multiform cadence of that space — with no shortcuts, and no frills. Just as a curve, the one right curve, defines the straightest line from Toronto to Barcelona.

★

There's another thing. I'm stymied when people have difficulty hearing polyphony on the page. Often they don't perceive how many shifts there are, how many tonalities are interlaced, till they hear it out loud. They never entered that cadential space; for them the real live poem, which is a many-voiced embodiment and a wooing, never began at all.

What were they hearing, I wonder, if they didn't pick up those gestures? Is it their ear or my music that was deficient?

★

I think I know how an open poem coheres, for all its bits and pieces. It's because, as the meditation moves through textured space, its changes of voice enact what I keep calling an articulate gesture of being. A lived coherence.

And that's because cadential space already lives through such movements. If you follow its grain, you find the poem achieving a fundamental gesture. Usually in spite of your preoccupations; sometimes against your will.

So you don't just stitch pieces together. The cadence you're trying to mime already enacts a fundamental gesture in the kinetic vocabulary of what is. Your job is to trust it.

★

And that's why meditative writing is also a letting be. You can't just whiz along in the prepackaged grids and grooves we impose on things to organize them. Or if you do you violate, you man-handle the torque and texture of the space you're writing in. You merely write a poem; you're a tourist, a small-time imperialist who imports his own right-angle inflections and tries to dig to Barcelona. Instead of following the grain of space and going the straight way round.

Which is why univocal poetry is so boring, and it feels like sacrilege. Even though it may be well written — a well written minification of what is. Most contemporary poetry *is* monophonic! Sure, the content changes. But all you carry away is that single stating voice, buzzing in your ear. And voice embodies being, and you hear the same monotonic news every time. The same reductive, claustrophobic blasphemy. And —

★

Sorry.

I need to make distinctions. A good monophonic poem — and it's true, such a thing exists — may mediate only one wavelength. But it mediates it well, without trying to utter things on other wavelengths which it can't encompass. And that will tell an honest partial truth.

What is unacceptable is the monophonic poem whose voice is badly cramped, and yet it insists on jamming the whole variegated world into its single, pygmy wavelength. I hate that kind of —

26.

This is phoney, you know.

Phoney? What are you talking about?

I've been carrying on as if it was me who makes up the tumble and slide on the page. And sure: I write the poem. But I don't *invent* the cadence I hear; I sit and play in the midst of it. Do you think I can boss it around? Most of the time I can't even keep up.

64

And don't you see? Those flexing voices — they *are* the poem. Without them, there'd be nothing: no weight, no resonance, just a batch of strung-together words.

That's the point of everything I've said. But I've made a farce of it. I've been talking as if you just crank out a meditation, as if you can reduce it all to the technical moves of the writer. As if you can tune out that magisterial cadence, and ignore its sponsoring presence in the poem. But that's a piece of shallow, modern bafflegab.

I wasn't expecting . . . Dennis, I'm sorry. But how else could we have gone at it?

I don't know. But it's not just how you assemble the poem, don't you see? That's only the outward part. The crucial thing —

27.

Cadence, and the mind-set of this era: they're incompatible. Cadence is something given, far greater than my own mind or craft, intimate, other, and which compels my awe. But the only analytic language for talking about it is the modern one — the poem as product of technique, the creative artist fashioning order from the raw material of the world or his own subconscious. I don't believe a word of it. Yet I'm a creature of modernity, and I still fall into the approach it's bred in us.

But that falsifies everything I know at the core. There has to be some way of talking about the two-way commerce between cadence and poem, not just analyzing the poem as a kind of vocal engineering job.

28.

The swivel and thrum I sense as perpetual, that I hear like a subsonic throbbing or the sea — even when I don't know I'm hearing it — I call "cadence."

It's what myself is turned toward, and homes to. Even though I'm so erratic in attending I wince to think about it.

In none of the senses I ever learned to use the word, I worship cadence.

★

I don't bow down before it. Partly because I can't locate an "it" to bow down "before." And partly because I tried that stance earlier in my life, and I always blew it.

But I do worship cadence, because there is nothing else you can do with it.

I used to think that in worship you worked up a frenzy of will and devotion. But this is so meat-and-potatoes, it's not like that at all. It is sheer attending, far beneath the threshold of your awareness. In astonishment, delight, trepidation, awe: knowing you're at home, knowing you're sullying it but that's how it is. And none of those things in a form you're even aware of.

I worship so inadequately that it sounds absurd to use the word. But that's the point. Good, bad, or indifferent, the quality of my response does not determine the magisterial hereness of cadence. And *that* is what elicits awe.

★

Why call it worship?

The response which cadence engenders is not curiosity; nor a desire to possess it (which would be ridiculous); nor to write about it; nor to take it apart and see what makes it tick; nor any other private motive. There is just impersonal stillness, and the elemental acknowledgement: cadence *is*, here, perpetual yes and we're in it. I don't understand what it means, that "cadence is." My head doesn't translate the knowing. But that doesn't bother me. If my head does its stuff with the fact some day, fine. And if not, that's fine too.

If I worshipped better, cadence would be no more real for that.

29.

I first became aware of these things in the way I described in "Cadence, Country, Silence." When I was in my twenties. I don't recall a sudden onset. It doesn't seem to me either personal or impersonal, though if I had to choose one term it would be the latter. Certainly I don't sit and talk to it; that's just not appropriate.

When the sense is strong, which for me isn't that often, you are so radically held — though there is almost no conscious awareness "of" cadence — that you are utterly concentrated. Without passing out or anything. It's hard to describe. It's not an extraordinary state; I've had my share of those, and they're far less trustworthy.

I don't try to work up the experience of cadence. I may try that with lots of things, but it doesn't apply here. Cadence continues; I'm just more thinly attuned at times. But when it does take over, the attending — in which there's no choice; the only choice would be *not* to attend, and barring an emergency in the house that would be ludicrous — the attending itself is what you're asked for. It feels like the first obedience that's enjoined. And it's scarcely "obedience," and you don't even feel "enjoined" . . .

This is ridiculous.

30.

There is also the writing. It's the fullest erotic response to cadence.

When cadence sifts through you, the invitation has already occurred. "Come and be part of me . . . Sit still, and be me."

What else can you do? You pick up a pen, and you try to reenact the inflections of that claim and courtship. To unfurl its gestures in your home medium.

Maybe that *is* the devotional discipline, I don't know. But it doesn't involve the effort of will that comes with doing your duty, nor what I thought worshipping God meant when I used to work at that. The only thing you can do is keep trying; you're lucky to get the chance. The problem isn't to make yourself do it, but to stop doing it long enough to lead the rest of your life.

31.

And what about the rest of your life?

It feels as if it is lived in the purview of cadence. There's nothing that isn't. But to my perplexity, I don't find any great effect in my day-to-day life. I don't trust that, since cadence seems so all-encompassing. But I have to report that my everyday behaviour, which is scrappy and compulsive and out-of-focus much of the time, doesn't seem to be modified by cadence.

Maybe there is some connection between cadence and the ethical, socially responsible, religious dimensions of life. There must be. But at my kindergarten stage, I haven't discovered what it is. At least not apart from the injunction to find words for the rich impossible space we live in.

That sets your vocation. For the rest, you muddle along.

32.

What is cadence up to?

It comes to me somewhat — with less of the utter knowing that cadence *is*; whatever it is — you couldn't dissuade me of that short of lobotomizing me — it comes to me sporadically, but then with some measure of that central knowing — it's not just a bright idea, it's a recognition of a truth surfacing beneath your own resources — that what is proceeding in cadence is the quick of what is.

Again, I don't know what that means. And I'm not terribly exercised to find out. Mostly it seems like something that is so, and whether I learn what it means or not is immaterial.

33.

Is it that the *structure* of what is is given in the kinetic forms
of cadence? . . . That sounds suspect.

Is it some *process* in the universe — some process *of* the
universe — that resounds in cadence?

A process one has gotten tuned into somehow, like a fluke
of reception on a shortwave radio.

I think it is. I think it's the process of be-ing. And if my use
of the word is obtrusive, I'm sorry. It's not an abstraction; it's
the most immediate word, it refers to the most immediate
thing there is about things. That they are at all, rather than
not being.

That's what you pick up in cadence.

34.

Cadence enacts the space of cosmos. "Cosmos," as what is.
And "space," as the still and tumultuous process in which
cosmos is perpetually recreated by the unspeakable energy of
be-ing — of *being at all*. To be tuned by cadence is to vibrate
with that calamitous resonance. And to write is to mime it,
polyphonically.

In this epoch, that is maybe how one speaks of it. In another
it might be different.

★

I don't believe I could persuade a reader of anything about
cadence.

My words are just a gesture of salute.

35.

All my poetry is a response to cadence. Maybe some of
the strangeness of what I write will diminish if a reader
perceives that. And that would please me. But it doesn't make
the poetry any better or worse to say these things. Indeed,

the poetry is finally by the bye; it depends on cadence, but cadence doesn't depend on it.

Which is why I was mortified, to speak of polyphony as if it were a matter of vocal engineering.

*

Cadence invites the poem to be. By being.

The poem reaches out to participate in that process.

Its polyphonic gestures enact the inflections of being wooed by, and wooing, the be-ing of what is.

PART TWO

The Poetry of Al Purdy

In 1944, at a cost of $200, Al Purdy engaged a printer in Vancouver to produce 500 copies of *The Enchanted Echo*, his first collection of verse. The author was less of an ethereal sprite than the title might imply, being lanky and rawboned in appearance, shambling and somewhat ornery in manner. His début did not attract widespread attention.

Purdy hailed from United Empire Loyalist country, the region of small towns and rolling farmland at the eastern end of Lake Ontario, where his forebears had settled in the 1780s. He was born there in 1918; his father, a farmer, died two years later. The son grew up in Trenton, in the care of his rigidly religious mother, and left school without completing grade ten. After drifting through occasional jobs, he joined the air force in 1940, and was now stationed in British Columbia for the duration of the war.

A less likely bard-in-the-making would be hard to imagine. And the fact is, Purdy would prove to be among the slowest developers in the history of poetry. For decades his progress consisted of false starts and apparently unproductive slogging. Only in retrospect can we discern the sureness of instinct which propelled him through his long apprenticeship, till he emerged as one of the fine poets of our time.

1. *The Long Apprenticeship*

Purdy had been writing verse since the age of thirteen, but in complete isolation from the central developments of twentieth-century writing. The modern poets he knew were those in his school anthologies: Kipling and Chesterton and Turner, Carman and Roberts and Pratt. And the poetry he wrote till he was past thirty is exemplified by the title piece from his book:

> I saw the milkweed float away,
> To curtsy, climb and hover,
> And seek among the crowded hills
> Another warmer lover.
>
> Across the autumn flushing streams,
> Adown the misty valleys,
> Atop the skyline's sharp redoubts
> Aswarm with colored alleys —
>
> I caught an echo in my hands,
> With pollen mixed for leaven —
> I gave it half my song to hold,
> And sent it back to heaven.
>
> Now oft, anon, as in a dream,
> O'er sculptured heights ascending,
> I hear a song — my song, but now,
> It has another ending.

With no other models available, this is where Purdy began. Why he didn't heed the advice he must have had in abundance — to find a job with a future, and stick to writing as a hobby — is beyond ordinary comprehension.

After the war Purdy found himself in Vancouver once more, where he worked in a mattress factory from 1950 to 1955. Then it was back east to Montreal for two years, to the fertile

and combative milieu that included Irving Layton, Louis
Dudek, Frank Scott, and Milton Acorn — Purdy by now
having resolved to make himself into a great poet. In 1957 he
and his wife built a small house on Roblin Lake, south of
Trenton. And there, with no cash, they settled in: Eurithe to
earn their keep, he to write. Albeit with an acute sense that
he had made nothing of his life so far, that perhaps he was a
permanent failure.

★

In 1960, to pause here at Roblin Lake, Purdy was forty-two.
He was reading omnivorously, and since 1955 he had published three chapbooks. He'd outgrown *The Enchanted Echo*. But
he still had not produced more than a handful of poems worth
keeping.

Some of the reasons for his slowness must lie in the inscrutable private rhythms of any writer's development. But from
the vantage of twenty-five years later, it is hard to resist the
conclusion that he was trying, however obscurely, to reinvent
modern poetry on his own terms. About 1952 he had been
goaded by a friend into reading the classics, particularly the
moderns. The effect was drastic. Consciously or not, he'd had
to accept that the formal tradition was bankrupt, at least for
his own imagination. Rhyme, metrical rhythm, fixed stanza
forms, and the stock poetical attitudes that Purdy had been
parading — these were drawn from a literary universe in
which the rough-hewn autodidact from Trenton could never
be more than an outsider. If he wanted to become his own
large clumsy aching generous eloquent awestricken self in
words, he would have to set aside the whole of traditional
poetry, start back at square one. In his mid-thirties, he would
have to recommence his apprenticeship in earnest.

And at that point, an apparently perverse spirit of independence had taken hold. He would not put himself to school
with the great modern masters: not Yeats or Eliot, not Pound
or Williams. Nor would he settle into one of the newer styles,
with Auden or Dylan Thomas. For better or worse he would

negotiate an independent passage — from the weird time warp of (say) 1910, where he'd been stuck, to his own here and now. But there was a price to pay for this stubbornness. Already a late developer, he would now have to spend another full decade catching up with himself.

Mind you, he did gain some momentum by wrestling with other poets. In the mid-fifties he wrote like Dylan Thomas for a year or two. And around 1958, he tried out Irving Layton's verbal flamboyance and self-assertive stance. But the results were more compacted and stiff-jointed than what he was reaching for, and soon he was pressing ahead again. What he needed was a way of writing that fitted him like a skin; that let him enact his own way of inhabiting the world, speak its native inflections. What his hands could touch, what his nerve ends knew — these would be the final test of words. Along with his inner ear.

A clear marker in the transition is the lively but exasperating "Gilgamesh and Friend," from 1959:

Eabani, or Enkidu, made by an itinerant goddess
From clay, hairy, perhaps human,
Destined to have carbuncles, goiter, fear of death —

Became friend of beasts, notable in that
He learned their language (played the flute?),
Was weaned from animals by a courtesan . . .
(How?) Joined Gilgamesh to initiate heroism
(First known ism?) in the Sumerian microcosm.
Killed bulls, wizards, monsters like Shumbaba

(Who had no genitals, thanks goodness!) in a cedar forest . . .

By now Purdy has started to loosen up. And the play of energy in the speaker's consciousness *is* the pent-up something that had been trying, all along, to find its way into his poetry. Letting that energy invade the process of composition — so that the poet simultaneously sketches his subject (like a musical

76

theme) and embroiders it with fancy honks and playful sup-
positions (like a series of improvised variations) — this looks
like the next step Purdy had to take . . . Except it isn't
working yet. The set stanza form just gets in the way, a residue
of alien convention. And the ostensible subject, Gilgamesh
and friend, disappears beneath the avalanche of wisecracks.

By 1960, dug in at Roblin Lake, Purdy was finally in motion.
But it still wasn't clear that he was going anywhere of poetic
interest.

★

What happened during the next two years was an abrupt
quantum leap, of the sort that defies explanation whenever it
occurs. In his collection of 1962, *Poems for All the Annettes,*
there are still misfires. But in the best poems, the mature
Purdy simply vaults free of three decades of marking time, in
a riot of exuberant, full-throated energy.

Now the closed forms of the past are spronged open with a
vengeance, releasing a headlong, sometimes dizzying cascade.
As in "Archaeology of Snow," where the line breaks and
phrasing seem configured by the play of unpredictable energy,
rather than being poured into a pre-existing mould:

Bawdy tale at first
                what happened
    in the snow
    what happens
                in bed or anywhere I said
                                oh Anna
            here —
                    here —
    here —
            here —
                    here — . . .

Once having discovered this degree of freedom, Purdy would
settle into a more restrained use of multiple margins and

spray-gun layout. But claiming such plasticity in the way a poem lands on the page seems to have been a necessary part of the breakthrough to his own voice.

And the *pace* of a poem is something he can control with virtuosity. Now certain line breaks occur after a word like "and" or "the" (dragging the reader on to the next line, to complete the unit of thought), while others coincide with a natural pause (recreating the breathers the imagination takes as it finds its way ahead). A canny modulation between these two kinds of line break was another sign of his maturing craft.

The poem has become an act of discovery for Purdy, rather than a list of things discovered. It's full of particulars. And it is fluid, constantly in process; often the lid is not quite banged shut at the end. Now he can catch a wide range of tonalities, from a headlong clatter to a delicate, murmuring equipoise: "Briefly briefly all things / make the sounds / that are theirs —." Or to the grave, almost liturgical hush of "Remains of an Indian Village":

> Standing knee-deep in the joined earth
> of their weightless bones,
> in the archaeological sunlight,
> the trembling voltage of summer,
> in the sunken reservoirs of rain,
> standing waist-deep in the criss-cross
> rivers of shadows,
> in the village of nightfall,
> the hunters silent and women
> bending over dark fires,
> I hear their broken consonants . . .

At forty-four, Purdy had come into his own — with all sirens going. The long apprenticeship was over. He had found his way to an open poetry which could be brash, adventurous, tender, self-mocking, sublime; within which he could move in any direction with gusto and abandon.

He had made the same journey, from a closed to an open poetic universe, that other major talents have accomplished in this century. But he'd done it in characteristically maverick fashion. He had refused to read Whitman, Pound, or Williams, whose free rhythms and vernacular diction would have made them obvious mentors. And he'd made temporary stopovers with Thomas and Layton, who were not pointing in the direction he would take at all. (D. H. Lawrence's poetry would soon become a touchstone for him — but only after 1965, when his own formation was complete.)

Purdy had found an independent path, to an unmarked destination, essentially by himself. And in the process he had become a genuine original.

★

In *The Cariboo Horses*, three years later, Purdy consolidated everything he had learned in the earlier leap and carried it further. There is now a wonderful sure-footedness in the rangy, loping gait which had become his signature — with its ability to open out into vast perspectives of space and time, then narrow down to a single moment or image. It was with this volume that he reached a wide critical and popular audience. And the spate of good and great poems began which have taken on normative status in our literature.

One advance was a new assurance in identifying his subject matter. For years I thought of *Cariboo Horses* as the book in which Purdy claimed his Canadian themes — perhaps because it includes "The Country North of Belleville," one of his first unequivocal masterpieces. But what's startling, on returning to the book, is how *much* of Purdy's home ground it claims. Here are the portraits, the vignettes, the early memories, poems of place, jokey breakneck yarns, on-the-spot reportage, har-de-har asides, delicate evocations of love and the natural world, broad satire, distant times and places: sex and death and poetry, the galaxy and Roblin Lake.

Above all, it's the book with the magisterial authority of lines like these:

Old fences drift vaguely among the trees
    a pile of moss-covered stones
gathered for some ghost purpose
has lost meaning under the meaningless sky
      — they are like cities under water
and the undulating green waves of time
      are laid on them . . .

                    ("The Country North of Belleville")

    With the appearance of *The Cariboo Horses*, in Purdy's forty-seventh year, this story of late-blooming, interminable, and heroic apprenticeship comes to completion. We need a different approach than the chronological to take the measure of the next three decades.

2. *The Process*

Surveying Purdy's mature poetry as a single body of work, stretching from 1962 to the present, reveals some large recurring features. One is the vision of *process* which informs his poetry. (I'll let the term gather its meaning as we proceed.)

    This vision is first of all historical. It's conceivable that growing up in Loyalist country (albeit with no great family stress on tradition) contributed to Purdy's sense of organic continuity in time. Certainly he has written often and well about the persistence of the past in that milieu. "Father and grandfathers are here," he says, "grandmothers and mother / farmers and horsebreakers / tangled in my flesh / who built my strength for a journey." ("In the Dream of Myself.") And in the two poems entitled "Roblin's Mills" he concentrates so hard on the nineteenth-century inhabitants of his town that he is granted contact with their lives, and communes with their "departures and morning rumours / gestures and almost touchings." Though they must subside again into the past, their continuity can now be gravely affirmed: "they had their being once / and left a place to stand on."

Even when the legacy of the past is indecipherable, that very message of obliterated purpose tells Purdy something about his roots. In "The Country North of Belleville," he meditates on inscrutable stone-piles and fences that no longer enclose anything, their farms long abandoned. And the choric lament rises in him: "This is the country of our defeat." Both the strength and the failures of the past live on in time.

★

For Purdy, time is a continuum that permits a commerce of dead with living, of living with dead — rather than being a wasteland, say, or an executioner. And so his sense of time passing is bittersweet, rather than merely bitter.

On the one hand, he laments what perishes. In "Elegy for a Grandfather," he expands on the old man's death to mourn for everything that dies:

> and earth takes him as it takes more beautiful things:
> populations of whole countries,
> museums and works of art,
> and women with such a glow
> it makes their background vanish
>   they vanish too,
> and Lesbos' singer in her sunny islands
> stopped when the sun went down —

Yet on the other hand, things don't just die. Thus he can remark (in "Temporizing in the Eternal City") on how "the past turned inside out / protrudes slightly into the present." Such continuity in time may not remove the scandal of transience and death, but it qualifies them in a nourishing way. Looking at the sculpture of Beatrice, he observes "something crouching there / joining the cadences of eternity."

★

So far, Purdy can be seen as having a sense of the partnership of human beings through time — as indeed he does. But to stop there would be to miss everything weird, wonderful, and distinct in his vision of space-time as a process.

We can glimpse this vision as early as "Night Song for a Woman" (perhaps his first fully mature poem, written in 1958). It's a mysterious little piece, truly a night song.

> A few times only, then away,
> leaving absence akin to presence
> in the changed look of
> buildings
>   an inch off centre —
>
> All things enter
> into me so softly I am
> aware of them
>   not myself
> the mind is sensuous
>   as the body
>   I am a sound
> out of hearing past
> Arcturus
>   still moving outward
>
> — if anyone were to listen
> they'd know
>   about humans

Something has happened to Purdy "a few times only, then away" — but what is it? The poem doesn't appear to say, though perhaps "All things enter into me" gestures at an answer. Again, how does Purdy suddenly find himself on this extraordinary jaunt out past Arcturus? And what is it that people would "know about humans" if they listened? Finally, on a very different tack: what enables these disconnected snatches to hang together at all? Palpably they do, in a breathless murmuring which seems suspended in eerie silence. But what is the source of their coherence?

We won't try to answer these questions yet. But it's evident that the universe according to Purdy operates on unfamiliar principles. It is not just that he can suddenly mutate into "a sound / out of hearing past / Arcturus / still moving outward" — but that the phenomenon is taken so casually for granted. Slipping across the galaxy is as much a matter of course as slipping across the street.

And once we recognize that, we can see that the same thing keeps happening — with all sorts of variations — throughout the whole of Purdy's work. Take a step in any direction and you find yourself in the nineteenth century, in long-ago Samarkand, in the Upper Cretaceous or outer space. The cosmos of Purdy's poetry is one in which familiar laws of movement in both space and time may be suspended without warning, and a different set of principles take over. A second or alternate universe is latent in the familiar one, and can assert itself at any time. What's intriguing is to chart the behaviour of this parallel reality — the cosmos of process.

★

In "Hockey Players," a game is suddenly detonated when three players swerve out of quotidian space, and into the alternate cosmos. They end up "skating thru the smoky end boards out / of sight and climbing up the appalachian highlands / and racing breast to breast across laurentian barrens." In itself, the moment is fanciful. But the underlying experience — of swerving out of the conventional world, and then covering ground so quickly that space collapses into a blur of simultaneity — is pure Purdy.

In "The Cariboo Horses," he watches cowboys riding into 100 Mile House on their "half-tame bronco rebels." He resists the impulse to romanticize the horses; yet even as he does he finds himself carried elsewhere and elsewhen, transfigured in contemplation of "the ghosts of horses battering thru the wind / whose names were the winds' common usage / whose life was the sun's." Only at the end of the poem does he return to the scene before him. It's a remarkable affirmation of parallel universes — of a day-to-day world, and a larger, more luminous one. And in the alternate universe, points far separated in space and time are simultaneous.

Again, standing "At the Athenian Market" Purdy moves into a kind of lucid trance. Now a pile of oranges is "involved with converging lines / of light Phidias the sculptor / laboured over half an hour / ago." And as the sight of the living girls in the marketplace carries him deeper into trance, he moves to union with "long ago girls" — and then, unexpectedly, further back still, to the first emergence of life from primordial waters, and to the very beginnings of evolution, "before these Greek cities / before the sea was named / before us all." Yet in truth Purdy doesn't even seem to be "moving back"; this is a stillness which goes beyond the wild canter of "The Hockey Players," and participates in other points in space-time without stirring an inch.

The poem is characteristic in that it sounds the note of lived, authentic exaltation precisely as it enters the aspect which seems the most remote from "real life" — that is, the intuition that all time and space are simultaneous. It's at this juncture that Purdy's poetry regularly takes on the nostril-flare or hush, and the quirky, kindled gait and diction, which make it irreplaceable — and which feel utterly unforced, at home in a mystery they know firsthand, "as the days and nights join hands / when everything becomes one thing." ("The Dead Poet.") The intuition feels more real than mundane reality.

The distant past juts into the immediate present; far away is near at hand. Space-time is plastic, elastic, fantastic. We don't yet know what that signifies. But there are examples by the hundred in Purdy's work; start reading with this in mind and it crops up everywhere, this "simultaneity of things / . . . the instant of the dinosaurs / whose instant I am part of." ("Lost in the Badlands.") The cosmos of process is close to being the primary universe of his poetry.

★

84

I have been speaking of Purdy's parallel cosmos, and referring to it as one of process. So far, the meaning of "process" seems to be mainly that a great deal of high-speed traffic goes on in the space-time continuum.

But there is more to it than that. For it is also characteristic of the process that it is chock-a-block with things which are incommensurable with one another, yet which coexist. Sometimes in discord, at other times flowing into one another. Time and again the poem presents, not a single reality which would enforce a single-keyed response, but that reality and its converse — or (more subtly) two or three further realities which chime off the first, in a discordant but richly complex music of being. That's how the world *is*. Nothing comes single; everything skids into the larger process, and by the very act of existing implicates its incommensurable brothers and lovers and foes and a joke and grandparents and death and the dinosaurs, not to mention intergalactic space and a hangover and spring and the first evolving rampant protozoa.

And the world provokes incompatible responses as a matter of daily course. Celebration and elegy simultaneously; or a fusion of raucous laughter, grief, and awe of an almost unbearable delicacy. Much of the energy of Purdy's work goes into delivering this Heraclitean flux intact. Our categorizing minds might prefer to keep segments of the world in airtight compartments. But the segments don't cooperate.

★

There are also poems in which the sense of simultaneity goes beyond the normal processes of time altogether. These are poems of ecstasy; they intuit an eternal *now*, in which every moment of past, present, and future participates, in some unfathomable way surviving its own disappearance.

Often Purdy moves into this ecstatic dimension as he contemplates the physical world, and finds himself held in a mysterious under-silence:

> in a pile of old snow
> under a high wall

a patch of brilliant
yellow dog piss
glows, and joins
things in the mind.
Sometimes I stand still,
like a core at the centre
of my senses, hidden and still —
All the heavy people,
clouds and tangible buildings,
enter and pass thru me:
stand like a spell
of the wild gold sunlight,
knowing the ache stones have,
how mountains suffer,
and a wet blackbird feels
flying past in the rain.
This is the still centre,
an involvement in silences —

("Winter Walking")

What is the meaning of this "rare arrival / of something entirely beyond us"? ("Time Past /Time Now.") Sometimes Purdy parses it explicitly as the moment in which things reveal their perpetual nature:

This incident:
            sitting with friends
in the chalet restaurant on top of Mount Royal
talking of a tree swaying back and forth in the wind,
leaving no silvery whip marks of its travelling self
            or proof of passage.
                        But we say
"That tree will always be there,
flogging the air forever." . . .

("Method for Calling Up Ghosts")

The intuition cannot be translated into conventional thought, of course. And Purdy is so suspicious of mystification of any

kind that he mostly backs away from pronouncements on the
subject, sometimes from doing anything more than pointing
to it cryptically. Often he contents himself with evoking the
feel of the eternal moment through the hush and susurration
of the words themselves:

> They are so different these small ones
> their green hair shines
> they lift their bodies high in light
> they droop in rain and move in unison
> toward some lost remembered place
> we came from like a question
> like a question and the answer
> nobody remembers now
> no one can remember . . .
>
> ("The Nurselog")

Mind you, to concentrate exclusively on these glimpses of
an eternal *now* is to create a one-sided version of the poetry.
Purdy is just as concerned with the horror and the boredom
of the world as with its murmurs of glory. But those murmurs
are worth identifying; they will help us to fathom what makes
the process cohere.

3. *Polyphony*

We move now to one of the most dazzling aspects of Purdy's
writing: his command of polyphony, his ability to orchestrate
many different voices. No reader can get through twenty lines
without becoming aware of the constant shifts of diction and
pacing and tone, the squawks and blips as Purdy's consciousness intrudes and recedes, the startling turnarounds from
redneck coarseness to a supple middle style to soaring passages of joy and lamentation. Purdy is one of the living masters
of voice.

And at this point, we can discern why "finding his voice"
was so difficult, and so crucial. The voice of his poems would
have to mime the nature of his subject matter — the process,

and himself in it. But the nature of the process is to be protean, chameleonic, constantly swerving and bucking and passing into its own opposite in the blink of an eye. Only when the voice of his poetry became as manifold and self-renewing as the process itself would Purdy be able to write the poems that beckoned him. He needed a polyvocal medium, one that could embody his sense of what the world is like.

It would be easy to present five quotations, or fifty, that speak in different voices. And that would indicate Purdy's astonishing tonal range. But it would not demonstrate the most important aspect of the matter — which is not simply that he uses different voices, often in the same poem, but that he's capable of shifting from one to the next in a seamless way, one that mimes a cosmos in which all things flow.

This is not the hard-edge mosaic technique of a Pound, say, where fragment A comes in one voice, fragment B in another, and the two are banged down side by side on the page with no transition. The technique of juxtaposing voices in a discontinuous mosaic issues properly from Pound's vision of things. It has been the main polyphonic tradition in this century; it has even been followed by poets who don't share Pound's vision, but who lack the stature to find their own way of writing polyphonically.

Purdy's technique, which lets him modulate seamlessly through a great range of voices, issues from *his* vision of the process. The resources of a poetry like this have not been extensively explored. Yet they are crucial to hearing his work on its own wavelength, and hence to understanding it at all.

To see how his polyphony works, we should examine the vocal trajectory of one poem from start to finish. To keep things manageable, we'll take a short piece.

Love at Roblin Lake

My ambition as I remember and
I always remember was always
to make love vulgarly and immensely

as the vulgar elephant doth
    & immense reptiles did
in the open air openly
sweating and grunting together
and going
    "BOING   BOING   BOING"
        making
every lunge a hole in the great dark
for summer cottagers to fall into at a later date
and hear inside faintly (like in a football
stadium when the home team loses)
ourselves still softly
    going
      "boing   boing   boing"
    as the vulgar elephant doth
      & immense reptiles did
in the star-filled places of earth
that I remember we left behind long ago
and forgotten everything after
on our journey into the dark

Consider the poem's broad movement in space-time. Purdy starts by conflating his own lovemaking with that of elephants and "immense reptiles," the latter presumably being the dinosaurs. There is already a fusion of times, though merely because the contemporary lover is wishing himself back to a more primitive past. But starting about line eleven, and then much more rapidly in the last four lines, there's an effect like an infinite camera pullback in a movie. Suddenly we see all the traffic of earth — the ambitious lover, the elephants, the long-ago dinosaurs, the planet itself — diminishing to the size of specks, as we unexpectedly pull away from them. This backwards zoom is taking place in time; we are receding into the evolutionary future, away from the "star-filled places of earth" (apparently a time-layer when humans still coupled with the unself-conscious instinct of beasts). And the pullback is also taking place in space; we are receding from the little planet earth into the intergalactic dark, where human and prehuman concerns are so far away they seem both infinitely small and infinitely poignant. The sense of bittersweet awe at the end is unnerving, especially since we have swerved such a great distance in so few lines.

What gives me goose bumps in this poem has to do, I believe, with the way the process of tonal change enacts the process being described. This is the larger truth about Purdy's poetry that we're after. He does not simply write *about* the process; he keeps miming it in the movement of the poem's voice, its vocal trajectory. Let's retrace "Love at Roblin Lake" with that in mind. For it is clear that the poem starts in one voice, and ends in another. But Purdy's skill at modulating voices is so great that it's far less clear how we got from one to the other.

The piece begins with the speaker as a bit of a bumbler, who gets himself tangled in words at the very outset: "My ambition as I remember and / I always remember was always . . ." After this abrupt little nosedive, the *grosseries* the speaker is about to deliver about making love "vulgarly and immensely" may give us a yuck or two, may even speak for the sweatily horny strain in us. But given the clumsy, almost coarse tone of his speaking voice, they seem unlikely to rise much above that level. (Few readers will be thinking any of this consciously as they proceed, of course. If the voice works, it will simply exert a tactful, preconscious pressure on our reading, setting the terms in which we experience the poem as a whole.)

The first surprise comes with the archaic "doth," which pops out at the mention of pachyderms and bygone dinosaurs. With that little tonal blip as the giveaway, the speaker now appears as a more sophisticated man: as one who enjoys playing roles, including that of a clodhopper — rather than simply *being* a clodhopper.

The description of rutting, complete with comic-book "BOING BOING BOING," picks up the note of har-de-har comedy again — only to dissolve into the weird, serpentine, but surprisingly persuasive image of the phallic trench as a hole in the dark which traps summer cottagers who turn out to be ourselves as well, now inside a football stadium and raising only muted cheers because the home team is losing. Wherever the poem is going, it's clearly nowhere we could have predicted at the start (a mere dozen lines ago). But the changing tone of the piece is itself guiding us through this free, uncharted trajectory in poetic space. By now the voice has become plain, yet sinewy and evocative; we have shifted away from the broad, slapdash tonality of the opening, and though it's not at all clear where we're headed, the voice now feels like a trustworthy guide.

Next we discover that we are both inside the stadium, making love and going "*boing*," and outside it, somewhere in undifferentiated space. And our increasing distance from the stadium action, our accelerating pullback, is mimed as the original "BOING BOING BOING" fades to "*boing boing boing.*" Now the vulgar elephant and the immense reptiles bear a kind of pathos of distance about them, as they echo their earlier appearance. And with the stammer of broken phrases which concludes the poem, we move into an eerie, hedgerow sublime. It may take a few readings before we can analyze where we are, physically or psychically — but at an emotional and imaginative level, the heart-wrenched, awestruck tone of the end has already told us:

> going
> "*boing boing boing*"
> as the vulgar elephant doth
> & immense reptiles did
> in the star-filled places of earth
> that I remember we left behind long ago
> and forgotten everything after
> on our journey into the dark

We are watching the funny, sexy, absurd, and poignant dance of mating, performed by one couple, by human beings, by all species that have dwelt on earth. We view them both from within the experience and from a remove that is some place like death, or eternity — where laughter, choked-back tears, and a cosmic hush commingle.

The changing trajectory of voice, together with the sweep of shifting perspectives, has helped Purdy to limn a process in which near and far, past and present, comic and tragic are somehow simultaneous.

4. *Tremendum*

We have a poetry characterized by zoom perspectives on space-time; by the simultaneity of things that don't jibe; by moments of luminous stillness; and by constant vocal shifts, which guide us through the process according to Purdy. What do they signify?

Purdy gives us a day-to-day world that is unmistakably the cranky, suffering, shades-of-grey place we inhabit. But at the same time he gives us an experience that keeps breaking through in moments of epiphany. This is an encounter with what theologians call *mysterium tremendum* — holy otherness. An appropriate response to the tremendum is awe, joy, terror, gratitude. We've seen a number of these ecstatic moments, where time seems to lock for the speaker, and the physical world is both utterly present and wholly transparent, a window into some ineffable dimension where he is at once lost and at home. There are many, many more.

For Purdy, such experience of tremendum is always mediated through things of the world. "My Grandfather's Country" ponders the way it impinges through place, and occurs with its own particularity in each locale. In the desert, for example, where "a man can walk and walk into identical distance / like an arrow lost in its own target." Or in the high Arctic, where:

> . . . there are seas in the north so blue
> that a polar bear can climb his own wish and walk the sky
> and wave on wave of that high blue washes over the mind
> and sings to each component part of the hearing blood

a radiance that burns down the dark buildings of night
and sings for 24 hours a day of long sea-days . . .

Frequently, as he says in "The Darkness," such experience
conveys "some lost kind of coherence / I've never found in
people / or in myself for that matter." Thus in "The Beavers
of Renfrew," he senses that the beavers still know,

the secret of staying completely still,
allowing ourselves to catch up
with the shadow just ahead of us
we have lost,
when the young world was a cloudy room
drifting thru morning stillness — . . .

And sensing this holy otherness in the daily world, he enters
the eternal *now*. Everything that has ever meant itself, ever
been at all, seems still to live undiminished in that dimension.
Hence everything is simultaneous with everything else — "as
if all we are / co-exists in so many forms / we encounter the
entire race / of men just by being / alive here." ("Archaeology
of Snow.")

This eternal *now* is not situated by Purdy anywhere specifi-
able: not in a heaven, nor an afterlife, nor art (though it can
mediate the intuition), nor his own mind (though it loves to
embroider the moment). He has no theories about it; all he
can do is recreate its onset on the page, magnificently, as direct
experience. Most of the time he scarcely seems to know what
to make of its incursions. And the religions which offer a
framework for the experience just make him snort atheisti-
cally. It's a pure, intuited condition which keeps barging into
the flux of the quotidian, without altering the mundane terms
in which he lives the rest of his life.

Purdy recreates the daily world as it appears in and out of
the light of tremendum. His life work, in all its variety, stands
as a series of responses to that central intuition.

And this makes sense of the distinctive elements of process
we have observed in his work. It explains the constant zoom

perspectives: to whirl from Roblin Lake to the early life of stone 200 million years ago — that is simply to mime the eternal *now*, in which all time and space are a dance of simultaneity. What's more, in that transcendent moment the heterogeneous things of the world coexist in a kind of charged coherence — without being forced into an abstract unity. So that is how he records them. And to let the poem's voice ripple through a spectrum of changes — that too is to mime the luminous flow in the tremendum, which daily things bespeak in their moments of glory.

That is, the jumps and segues in his poems, their insistence on overlaid or clashing realities, their polyphony — these take their deepest origin from the intuition of *mysterium tremendum* in the day-to-day world. Purdy's unique way of moving in a poem, and of orchestrating its elements, derives from his fundamental vision of what the world is like. Which is to say, his artistry is mature.

*

Providing the term is kept free of associations with dogma and churchy attitudes, this vision is properly called religious. But Purdy still doesn't pretend to know what it *means* that such incandescence lurks in the quotidian. The experience is indelible; its significance is opaque. Questions about God or immortality receive no answer from within the process. The tentative prayer in "The Darkness" is about as close as he's let himself come to addressing the "spirit of everyplace / guardian beyond the edge of chaos" as though it could hear him. And it would be the cheapest effrontery on a reader's part to march in and explain this impulse in his poetry. Or baptize it. Or even label it possessively. My terms for it, "tremendum" and "the eternal *now*," are meant to honour the mystery, not straitjacket it. And the ecstatic power and incandescent grace which the poetry takes on as it enters the kinetic stillness furnish all the validation that I, for one, could ask.

*

But Purdy frets at times that he may be simply projecting the movements of his own mind onto the world. "I mistrust the mind-quality that tempts me / to embroider and exaggerate things." ("The Horseman of Agawa.") And it's true; sometimes he himself is clearly inventing the wild leaps which a poem enacts. The result can be a willed, rather frantic exercise.

But the tall tales and goofy exaggerations don't pretend to be anything other than that. And far from calling in question his deeper treatment of the process, they seem like a coltish retracing of what his intuition already knows. For Purdy writes from a profoundly intuitive imagination, which can tap into some ache and transcendence at the heart of things, and kindle in response. The ecstatic passages of "My Grandfather's Country," "The Beavers of Renfrew," "Night Song for a Woman" — these unmistakably touch grace, whatever its name may be. As do dozens of others. Entering these moments in the poetry, we sense a great hush which sustains the disparate things that are, and renders their all-over-the-map simultaneity and their vocal flow coherent. Such moments don't seem willed by the poet; they seem sponsored by being.

★

But to end on that lofty note would convey a false impression — not of the vision which animates Purdy's poetry, but of the poems themselves. For one thing, they often report on a daily world which shows no trace of tremendum, and which can be unrelievedly brutal at times. Some of these more humdrum pieces are vigorous and engaging; others are just prosy. But that merely shows that Purdy spends much of his time in a middle state, like the rest of us. He doesn't have nonstop entry to the cosmos of process.

Of greater interest is the compulsion he feels to avoid giving even a sublime poem too much polish, too final and finished a surface. There is an offhandedness, even a slapdash quality, which is clearly an intrinsic part of the way he wants a poem to *be*. That this is a deliberate policy is evident if we examine his revisions. They can go on for years, decades even, and frequently they polish individual passages to a burnished glow. But often the piece as a whole is left with an in-process, written-while-experienced feel to it; sometimes revision takes it further in that direction. This is an imagination which refuses to be housebroken. And if we approach even a classic Purdy poem too reverently, expecting a rarified masterpiece, it's likely to light a cigar, tell a bad joke, get up and leave halfway through the conversation. The high style comes and goes as it pleases — as at the end of "Spring Song":

> someone breathed or sighed or spoke
> and everything rearranged itself
> from is to was the white moon tracks
> her silver self across the purple night
> replacing time with a celestial
> hour glass halfway between a girl
> and woman I forgot till she comes jiggling
> back from the dark mailbox at last migawd
> hosanna in the lowest mons veneris I
> will never get to change the goddam oil

Purdy is a plain man visited by towering intuitions, not a beatified mystic. And his loose-jointed, bantery middle style affords a complex artistic leverage. It lets him acknowledge the long dry stretches between epiphanies — by the very act of including that middle voice. It gives him a way of honouring his plebeian origins, as his highfalutin early verse did not. And it provides a kind of ground bass, against which the moments of tremendum can register more tellingly when they come along. If he does connect with one of those incandescent moments, it will enter a poem whose voice can then modulate or erupt — thanks to his immense improvisational talents — into the high style of the epiphany, and thereby reenact the process it records.

This vocal strategy accounts for much of the unique temper and form of Purdy's work. The trick for a reader is to settle onto a wavelength that can accommodate, as they occur, both the consciously rough-hewn textures *and* the inflections of the incandescent. Purdy has in effect redefined "a poem" to mean a piece of writing that plays in the space between those boundaries — never in the same way twice. Across the body of his work, that changing vocal play is what we're invited to enjoy.

5. *Native Speaking*

There are other critical approaches that illuminate Purdy's work. I'll take one more here, considering his poetry as a venture in native speaking.

For half a century, Purdy has been lugging a preoccupation with the spirit of place back and forth across his homeland. The result has been a series of poems about locales and events which assemble into an imaginative map of Canada — not an exhaustive one, but far more complete than any other writer's. Without itemizing individual poems, we can say that he has followed the path of firsthand exploration described in "Transient":

> after a while the eyes digest a country and
> the belly perceives a mapmaker's vision
> in dust and dirt on the face and hands here
>
> . . .
>
> and the shape of home is under your fingernails
> the borders of yourself grown into certainty

These poems of Canadian place and history are a grand gift to the rest of us.

Purdy has "placed" us in subtler ways as well. For one thing, the imaginative journeys he has taken elsewhere in space-time coalesce into a larger map: this time, an experiential record of what one man has discovered in the universe. (I have in mind his journeys to other times and species, along with the literal globetrotting.) It makes no pretence to being a scholarly world history; the mapmaker's vision is still perceived in the belly and under the fingernails. But the vistas of geological time and interstellar space within which Purdy ranges are breathtaking. And because everything he encounters can be charged with tremendum, can reveal itself as part of the luminous process, his record of journeys in the universe stands as a poetic cosmology, an account of meaningful order.

What's notable is that Purdy focuses the cosmos from the vantage point of his own home. Sometimes this is explicit; in "News Report at Ameliasburg" he transmits a cacophony of war reports from global history, then winds down with a report on sunset in his own small village. But with or without the explicit reference point, a Canada-centred relationship of "there" to "here," of "then" to "now" is defined right in the idiom and perspective of the speaker, who is unmistakably a contemporary Canuck by the name of Al Purdy.

And now there is a new thing on earth: a poetic cosmology focused concentrically around Roblin Lake, southeastern Ontario, Canada, North America, planet earth, all space-time. It does not invalidate visions of order centred elsewhere. But here is a body of major poetry — a muscular, roomy, and persuasive vision of coherence — centred in our own here and now. Such a thing did not exist before.

*

To write as a native speaker is not just a matter of exploring Canadian places and deeds, however, nor even of mapping the world with Canada as the imaginative centre. At a deeper level it is to embody in words our historic modes of dwelling here — not by describing them at arm's length, but by enacting them on the page. And Purdy has articulated our native reflexes and tensions right in the musculature and movement of his poems. That too has opened imaginative room for us to dwell in.

It would take a whole further essay to explore Purdy's work from this perspective. But let me identify at least some of the native reflexes which inform his work. No one of them is uniquely Canadian, but taken together they have much to do with who we've been here.

The first concerns the tremendum. Throughout history, many things have served as the vehicle for encounter with holy otherness: sexual love, battle, religious contemplation, for example. It is central to our history and imagination in this part of the world that we approach the tremendum through knowing the vast, extreme and eerie land we inhabit. The mystique is strong even among confirmed city dwellers. And Purdy's poems of the land embody that reflex to a singular degree.

A second native reflex is that of instinctively locating our fragile human settlements, even the big cities, in a surrounding space of almost inconceivable magnitude, and as tenuous moments in a field of time which loops back at once to Stone Age humans and out through intergalactic light years. For that *is* the nature of our dwelling here. The land is vast. Much of the ground our feet or tires traverse was formed eons ago. And the time of white settlement is such a thin patina, usually less than two hundred years in depth, that once we penetrate even a hair's breadth beyond it we are swept into vast reaches of human and prehuman time. In Purdy, that sense of our dwelling contributes to the deep, frequently joyous reflex of temporal and spatial hopscotching that we've already observed.

In "The Runners," a speaker declares, "I think the land knows we are here, / I think the land knows we are strangers." That seems to me the paradigm of a third reflex — a deep and positive ambivalence in the Canadian makeup, which resonates across many aspects of our lives. "The land knows we are here." It antedates us, exerts a claim upon us, and somehow makes us welcome if we come to it knowing our place. We are not free simply to master and remake it according to the dictates of our own wills, as has been a dominant American pattern. We are free to belong to it, gingerly. Yet "the land knows we are strangers." We do not have a history of countless generations here, in which we have domesticated nature and can feel safe in its interpenetration with civilization — as did our forebears in Europe. Both declarations are true to who we are. We exist in their continuing tension, in

99

which we are compelled by both the Old World and the American version of the New — yet neither feels like us. It is a destiny of incomplete or multiple answers, of irony, of perpetual lack of full definition. Purdy's poetry, with its grand articulation of being both strange and at home in this place — a sensitive brawler in taverns, a learnèd rube — embodies that tension in its very fabric.

A fourth reflex has to do with eloquence, delicacy of feeling, amplitude of spirit. It is central to our social and cultural heritage that these things can be expressed, but only if they are cloaked in defensive irony. And once they *have* been revealed, we hear them echoing in a still vaster silence, and subsiding into it very quickly again. Purdy's poems enact that reflex, time and again, in their emotional trajectory.

In its embodiment of these deep, historic modes of being here, his poetry articulates who we are — places us in our home space — to an unprecedented degree. In speaking of this, of course, we can't homogenize all Canadians into a single mould. People with other modes of dwelling engrained in their marrow are no less Canadian for that. But whether or not we like every reflex the poems embody, they *are* many of us. And so we can move through this poetry without having to turn ourselves into denizens of somewhere else, merely to follow its natural lines of movement. At this profound, almost preconscious level, Purdy is a supremely accomplished native speaker.

6. *Purdy's Stature*

How are we to assess Al Purdy? It seems to me incontrovertible that he is among the finest living poets, and one of the substantial poets in English of the century. Of the hundreds of poems he has published, some fifteen or twenty place him in the rank of poets like D. H. Lawrence, Robert Frost, Dylan Thomas, Robert Creeley. If we have to realign our notion of what great poetry looks like to accommodate his best work — and it's part of his achievement that we do — that is scarcely a novel experience when a writer of stature comes along.

There's something more as well. If we step back several paces, we can find a broader perspective in which to situate Purdy, one that sheds fuller light on his achievement.

From the sixteenth century on, the imperial nations of Europe spread their languages and cultural paradigms around the planet: English, French, Spanish, Portuguese, and to a lesser extent Dutch. For better and worse. And during the twentieth century, after a long colonial period, literature in those languages became polycentric, as the former colonies found their voices — rivalling and sometimes surpassing the imperial centres. The most impressive contemporary example is that of Spanish and Portuguese writing in Latin America, but the process has been repeated around the globe, in recent decades with gathering potency.

This has not just been a matter of poets and novelists in the ex-colonies learning to write well in the fashion of their erstwhile mentors. The language of the metropolitan imagination has had to be unlearned, even as it was being learned from. A long hard struggle of independence has been necessary for writers of the hinterlands to imagine their own time and place, to become articulate as native speakers. The titans have been those who first broke through to indigenous articulacy, who subverted and recast the forms of the metropolitan imagination so as to utter the truths of the hinterland. Generally they've done so with a rare fusion of high artistry and folk, even populist imagination. It's clear that Whitman, Melville, Neruda, García Márquez are among the founders who've claimed a nation's patrimony this way, and in the process recast the imaginative vocabulary of their medium. Without pretending to exhaustive knowledge of the subject, I suspect their number also includes Darío, Amado, Guillén, Asturias, Césaire, Miron, Senghor, Walcott.

In the case of countries colonized by England, the situation is complicated one stage further. American writers made their breakthrough to native speaking very early, in the nineteenth century. In the result, American literature went on to such strengths that by the mid-twentieth century, anglophone writers elsewhere had to free themselves from the hegemony of both Britain and the United States. Such a situation does not exist in French, Spanish, or Portuguese. But that anomaly recognized, the challenge of speaking native among English-speaking writers in Africa, India, Canada, Australia, the Caribbean, and elsewhere has been parallel to that faced by a Neruda or a Senghor.

And that situates Al Purdy in a wider context. He has been one of the giants of the recurrent process in which, language by language and country by country over the last seventy years, the hinterlands of empire have broken through to universal resonance by learning to speak local. Purdy has claimed, and in many ways created, an indigenous imaginative patrimony for English Canada.

To say that is not to denigrate Canadian poets whose excellence is of other kinds — Irving Layton and Margaret Avison, for a start. Emily Dickinson wasn't called to be Whitman, nor Vallejo Neruda. But in his rootedness, his breadth, and his impulse to forge a native idiom for the imagination, Purdy is one of a distinct breed: the heroic founders, who give their people a voice as they go about their own necessities.

Of course, not all giants are equal in stature. And seen in that lofty company, Purdy may be one of the lesser titans. But it is among their number that he must be counted.

★

It is a matter of fact that readers abroad have scarcely begun to discover Al Purdy. Or more accurately, have not yet taken the crucial first step — of hearing this hinterland idiom on its own wavelength, as an instrument capable of genius, at once familiar and foreign. But such tone-deafness in the metropolis is an old story. It is the hard luck of London and New York, which time will rectify.

Meanwhile, for those who can read Purdy on his own wavelength, his poetry is a windfall and a blessing.

Acts of Dwelling, Acts of Love

> . . . the random testimony gathered
> as best we can, each of us down
> to essentials, as the failed are
> and the dead, who bear us forward
> in their fine, accurate arms.

A wonderful poet is gone. Bronwen Wallace, whose recent work is among the fine achievements of Canadian poetry, has died of cancer. She was forty-four.

Readers and critics are still catching up with this remarkable woman, who went from anonymity to artistic maturity on fast forward. Her first, apprentice collection came out in 1980, when she was thirty-five. By the next book, three years later, she was writing as her own woman. And with *Common Magic* (1985), and especially *The Stubborn Particulars of Grace* (1987), a unique voice was in full spate. There's nothing quite like it in contemporary poetry.

She wrote with humane gusto, a large-spirited feminism, and a deeply innovative approach to storytelling. Yet her craft doesn't point to itself; it's there to reveal the ordinary, luminous lives she portrays. If Alice Munro wrote poetry, you feel, this is what it might sound like.

★

A friend tells of visiting Bronwen in Kingston last spring, before the cancer showed up. It was a warm Saturday, and they set out on a five-minute stroll to the farmers' market. An hour later, they still hadn't arrived. Every block or so Bronwen would be hailed by a friend or relative, often a generation older, with whom familiar stories had to be savoured, recent news and gossip updated. Merely going from A to B in her own hometown, she was tacking through currents of tribal narrative.

It was if they'd walked into one of her poems. "Geography and place are extremely important to me," she told the literary magazine *Arc* in an interview last year. "And how we tell the stories of our lives, how we chart our way through life, is important. Those two things are really connected for me."

She came by that linkage of story and place honestly. Bronwen spent all but eight years of her life in Kingston. Her mother's family was United Empire Loyalist; her father's had lived on the same farm for almost two hundred years. With that background, she found southeastern Ontario — the towns, the great lake, the rolling farmland — a geography of stories, from which she drew hungrily. She once referred to these stories as "what I have to call a country."

It made her work crackle with an energy that feels more than just literary. A recent poem may be two, three, even four pages long, packed with narrative detail. And it rambles. It's a lopey, loopy canter through domestic vignettes, childhood memories, snatches of yarning and yack with women friends, plus alternate takes and digressions, all hopscotching through lives and generations linked in a rich random tapestry, maybe punctuated by notions picked up from neurology or prehistory, with the whole lit up by passages of luminous musing on the workaday mystery of being human.

It's like a segment of that composite narrative on the walk to the market. Without quoting half a dozen poems, it's hard to convey the overall effect: the sheer meditative grace of these crazy-quilt structures, which accommodate everything *and* the kitchen sink — yet manage to soar. I used to wonder, as Bronwen grew looser and more daring with each book, how the poems could achieve such glowing coherence. Why didn't they just fly apart? Now I think it's because, as a poet of place, she was never just a purveyor of local colour. She was a poet of nesting, of dwelling. No matter how private or diffuse the details, her poems became rituals of claiming her habitation.

That's what the stories are for — to uncover, in her own time and place, the lineaments of home.

In one such poem (one of the more straightforward, as it happens), she coaxes out the hidden dimensions of the lives surrounding her:

Common Magic

Your best friend falls in love
and her brain turns to water.
You can watch her lips move,
making the customary sounds,
but you can see they're merely
words, flimsy as bubbles rising
from some golden sea where she
swims sleek and exotic as a mermaid.

It's always like that.
You stop for lunch in a crowded
restaurant and the waitress floats
toward you. You can tell she doesn't care
whether you have the baked or the french-fried
and you wonder if your voice comes
in bubbles too.

It's not just women either. Or love
for that matter. The old man
across from you on the bus holds
a young child on his knee; he is singing
to her and his voice is a small boy
turning somersaults in the green
country of his blood.
It's only when the driver calls his stop
that he emerges into this puzzle
of brick and tiny hedges. Only then
you notice his shaking hands, his need
of the child to guide him home.

All over the city
you move in your own seasons
through the seasons of others: old women, faces
clawed by weather you can't feel
clack dry tongues at passersby
while adolescents seethe
in their glassy atmospheres of anger.

In parks, children
are alien life-forms, rooted
in the galaxies they've grown through
to get here. Their games weave
the interface and their laughter
tickles that part of your brain where smells
are hidden and the nuzzling textures of things.

It's a wonder that anything gets done
at all: a mechanic flails
at the muffler of your car
through whatever storm he's trapped inside
and the mailman stares at numbers
from the haze of a distant summer.

Yet somehow letters arrive and buses
remember their routes. Banks balance.
Mangoes ripen on the supermarket shelves.
Everyone manages. You gulp the thin air
of this planet as if it were the only
one you knew. Even the earth you're
standing on seems solid enough.
It's always the chance word, unthinking
gesture that unlocks the face before you.
Reveals the intricate countries
deep within the eyes. The hidden
lives, like sudden miracles,
that breathe there.

So these reports from a provincial town are never just parochial. Her final book took its epigraph from Flannery O'Connor: "Possibility and limitation mean about the same thing." By hunkering into the lives and stories that defined *this* particular place, she achieved a universal gesture of being human. Her poems were acts of dwelling, acts of love.

★

Wallace became the poet of her own place; she also became the poet of her own sex. You can feel her delight in releasing the secret, bottled-up stories of women.

Thus she explored the lives of her female forebears, some thriving in a patriarchal world, some going under. She wrote about girlhood, giving birth, being a mother. Quite wonderfully, about the nurturing friendship of women. And in two scarifying batches of poems, she wrote about what she'd seen at Interval House, a shelter for battered women in Kingston where she worked for two years. She was one of many literary pioneers of "female content"; she happened to be among the most vital and humane.

But there was more to her literary feminism, and here she had fewer companions. In the *Arc* interview, she spoke about what she'd learned from Al Purdy. His example gave her permission "to structure my poems in the form of a narrative, when every other woman I knew was writing lyrics." And she went on, intriguingly, "I see my talent in taking what is ostensibly a narrative form, and by giving it a female voice I think I change its shape and direction."

What did she mean by that?

In traditional narrative form there is a unified story, which unfolds with a beginning, middle, and end. But in the past century writers have explored other possibilities — both because our lives are seldom that tidy, and because other ways of telling a story are galvanizing too. Bronwen's exploration of "female narrative form" was one such experiment. Her innovation was to organize poems with a characteristic form women use when they tell each other stories. This unofficial tradition of storytelling is something most men notice only long enough to walk around it, while women know it so intimately they might never describe it as a tradition. It's the common female practice of telling each other yarns from their daily experience, continuously, as they occur. It amounts to imagining their own lives, outside official codes of meaning. Replaying them orally, scrutinizing them with a friend to find their emotional meaning. Such a personal narrative is never finished, because there's always another instalment to be lived and recounted.

This is a very different model of storytelling from the high-art kind. When two women take up their shared narration — on the bus, over coffee, on the phone — they're already aware of the major plotlines. For one, it's the dumb colleague or boss, the new man in her life, the operation; for the other, the dying mother, the sick child, the restless husband. So at each session they dive straight into updates, with no sign of a formal beginning. Nor are there many endings, since the story always breaks off at the point the narrator has reached in her life today. Mostly the plots consist of vivid, unresolved middles.

And if the story is seldom complete, neither is it unified. The new episode from one plotline tumbles out chock-a-block with new episodes from all the others. Often the narrators perform virtuoso feats of jump-cutting, which leave anyone who overhears completely dizzy. And so the structural principles of this narrative are digression, interruption, free association, cross-weaving, speculation, reexamination. ("Wait a minute; did he say 'when he leaves his wife,' or 'if he leaves his wife'?")

The real narrative is the cumulative stream of all the stories told: past, present, and future. So long as the protagonists are alive, what matters is not the shape discovered in the flow during any one session, but the ongoing process itself, of narrating their lives as they live them.

This is a folk-art form. For a sophisticated writer to adopt it as a structural model must have called for some nerve. But reading Bronwen's later work, it seems to me unmistakable: much of her energy went into creating a new poetic instrument — "female narrative form" — and learning to play it. Not that she transcribed actual conversations, of course. It was a matter of claiming for poetry the freedom to orchestrate chunks of separate story lines into a larger whole. There have been analogous experiments in fiction. But in poetry, be it Canadian or international, no one else had tried some of the things she was doing.

The music that's unique to Bronwen Wallace is sometimes there in the language — but always, and prodigally, in the form. By the time of *The Stubborn Particulars of Grace*, the results were dazzling.

★

There are other stories to tell about Bronwen, and they break your heart. Of the wife and mother. Of the poet who finished her first book of stories just before she died. Of the woman loved by a circle of female friends, many of them poets; the writer who galvanized students and younger writers with her earthy, unstinting assistance.

All those stories have ended too soon. But at least we have the work of her early prime, which is fully achieved. Bronwen Wallace left a total of some 130 poems. The best join the stock from which the living will draw nourishment for generations. They help to trigger

>*that spark in a synapse somewhere . . .*
>*saying* look, you have time, even yet
>to come to love this too.

Judy Merril Meets
Rochdale College

In August 1968 Judy Merril made a brief detour to Toronto. She wasn't coming as the noted writer and anthologist of speculative fiction, but as a frustrated political animal. She had been at the Democratic convention in Chicago, searching for a revolution to join. If it materialized, she told herself, she would remain in the States and dig in. But nothing she'd seen had convinced her. Now she was driving back to Pennsylvania; then it would be on to England, perhaps to stay. Vietnam mattered, and civil rights mattered. But the frantic burnout of the American Left was too much to cope with.

On impulse, she crossed the border for a day's visit with Chandler Davis, a mathematician and activist who taught at the University of Toronto. He pointed out a new educational experiment, Rochdale College, which was to be housed in a cooperative student residence near the university. The building itself, a high-rise tower on Bloor Street, would open that September.

What Rochdale would *be* was still a blur. But the founding statement touched a chord in Judy. No entrance requirements; no preset courses; no degrees. No hierarchy of staff and students. And an open invitation to reinvent the forms of knowing — not just in seminars, but by imaginative work, political action, crafts. Judy was forty-five, and hungry for a serious challenge. She went back to Pennsylvania to take stock. And in November 1968, after an epic all-night drive, she installed herself in an Aphrodite Suite at Rochdale College.

She planned to stay for a year, while she worked out permanent plans.

And here we are, a quarter century later, celebrating one of our own: this protean, questing, clear-eyed, prophetically non-cozy, leather-lunged, wisecracking, almost overpoweringly good-hearted literary broad in running shoes.

★

That was a larger-than-life encounter: *Judy Merril Meets Rochdale College*. I was there for it, and I observed it with awe. And I believe you can discern much of what Judy is about by pondering the three years she ploughed into her new home. Though to do so, we have to take a step back.

Rochdale was something else. In fact, it was a whole series of something elses. The building itself was the showpiece of the student co-op movement, which had proven to newly bulging Ontario universities that students could often house themselves better than the universities could. Meanwhile, Rochdale's education project was the brainchild of a group of U of T staff and graduate students, who couldn't abide the increasing superficiality and career orientation there. No two had the same notion of what the ideal university would look like. But they'd dreamed up "Rochdale College" as a neutral yet supportive framework, where people could work out their various educational destinies in a more challenging way than the university permitted.

This was quixotic enough. But what Judy walked into that November had already been hijacked by history, leaving the original vision miles behind. There had been a first year of sorts in 1967–68, with about a hundred people involved. And now the building was open — still unfinished, but replete with 850 residents (some full-time at Rochdale, most enrolled as students elsewhere). As well, there were hundreds of external members, and still more casual visitors. Government was to be by all participants, their average age being perhaps twenty-two. And so there were several thousand agendas in play. As they crisscrossed, miscegenated, cancelled one another out, the building practically lifted off Bloor Street, turning into a surreal mix of battle zone and garden of earthly delights.

And that was just the beginning. For though no one planned it this way, the building had opened right after the first full summer of the counterculture in Toronto. Hippies and diggers and heads had converged on Yorkville — to the astonishment of everyone else in the city, who had never seen such a thing. Not in Toronto! And then the weather changed. Soon a beeline of chilly freaks was trundling the five blocks west to Rochdale, hungry for higher education, or at least for a place to crash. What's more, the flower children overlapped with a second unexpected contingent: a healthy cross-section of the draft dodgers who'd recently arrived in the city, their basic take on things shaped by the American apocalypse of the sixties. And then a third wave appeared: a more ragtag, troubled procession of teenage runaways, drifters, drug dealers, and bikers.

Not that the problems surfaced at once. I had taught four years at the University of Toronto, and then served as a resource person at the pre-high-rise Rochdale. When the building opened that fall, I had never seen so many gifted, passionate, committed people in one place. The first month was a nonstop adrenalin high. The millennium was taking hold!

Which explains the carnival Judy encountered when she arrived. There was a drama group in the basement; as Theatre Passe Muraille, it would soon help recast the whole idiom of the English Canadian stage. Somebody was building a laser (or was it a phaser? a maser?) with found parts. There were seminars posted in Hebrew conversation, integral structural systems, urban revolution, De Fat Daddy Discontinuous Narcotics Cinema Permanente, Heidegger and phenomenology. Coach House Press was in residence in the back lane, cranking out mindblowing poetical whatzits; House of Anansi was humming two blocks away. To put it as modestly as possible, Western civilization was being recreated at the corner of Huron and Bloor.

At the same time, there was a babel of contradictory visions of Rochdale. Increasingly these had to do with how people should coexist in the building, less and less with establishing projects or seminars. Leafing through old copies of the Rochdale *Daily Planet*, I'm carried back to that hubbub of rival visions. This was all about creating a high-rise commune. *Wrong!* it was about reconciling the freaks and the straights. *Wrong!* it was about empowering the crasher proletariat. It was about creating a place to regress in, to go sane by falling apart. It was about learning a little consideration for others . . .

And then, as I turn the pages, the plaintive or wrathful notices begin to multiply. Why don't the garbage chutes work? When will the elevators start again? (The building was eighteen storeys high.) Who's *running* this place? Crashers have rights! Security measures. Small acts of kindness. The principled midnight theft of the front-door locks — were we going to recreate the repressive structures of capitalist society? An entire council impeached. The chess ladder flourishing. "*Attention: The Narcotics Police are poised to invade!*" (And a week later, "*Attention: The Bikers are poised . . .*" — hell, *somebody* was poised to invade!) Guns and the Rochdale day care. Overdue rents. Bad acid. Mass evictions. Freakouts & suicides. The media baying.

It would have taken someone comfortable with simultaneous alternate realities to flourish in that brave, indulgent, destructive cacophony. Someone with an instinct for multidimensional human chess: a delight in watching systems and countersystems tumble through their changes. And not at a safe theoretical remove, but tangled in working dreams and lives.

I was not that someone. In fact, I was shell-shocked. One month into the building's life and I'd become history — a nerdy troglodyte from the far-off, risible days of university reform. By mid-November I was ghosting around the place like a zombie. I strongly suspected this was not my scene.

*

Which explains my awe at the way Judy arrived. Here was a woman who took to the flow like a denizen: riding the energies, playing the riffle-shuffle of visions and paradigms as if one of her own SF anthologies had come to life around her. And she did it with gusto. Whatever I understood by the word "Rabelaisian" took on new texture as Judy bestrode the lobby or the second-floor common room, lopsided grin at the ready, glee in her eye. "What can you show me?" On the prowl for whatever unlikely encounter *this* quarter-hour would bring. She wasn't just coping with the hairy, incommensurable variety. She was surfing it!

What did she do? One of her first acts was revealing. The day after she arrived, she took a look around and realized the place was in total anarchy. The question was, why hadn't it fallen apart? As a simpleminded newcomer, she figured the maintenance staff must be as strategic as the administration. So she checked it out — and met a budding nuclear physicist, a Tai Chi devotee with a PhD, a general grab bag of mensches. Amid the din of two thousand hyperventilating strangers, she had located a solid energy centre; within half an hour, she'd bonded with them . . . And that was Judy.

What else? A bare listing of her first-year activities makes my head spin. She cofounded "Red, White, and Black," a counselling group for American dodgers and deserters. A lot of her energy went into the Rochdale Medical Clinic (which her daughter Ann had initiated). Seeing how few seminars were achieving continuity, she started and helped staff the Pub, a publication centre where you could print things yourself. She set up a library, donating thousands of her own books and periodicals. She was an earthy bohemian drill sergeant at council meetings, calling for ethical directness. ("If we have to evict the speed freaks, we can at least do it without hypocrisy.") She staged a science-fiction festival, featuring Samuel Delany, Frederick Pohl, Fritz Leiber, Ed Emshwiller.

And on and on it went. Rochdale had met Judy Merril.

★

But a list of separate projects doesn't tell the tale, because it's the *shape* of the thing I'm after. And in tracing the larger picture of Judy at Rochdale, I believe we also descry the science-fiction pioneer, and the communal activist who has enriched life in Canada, Japan, and Jamaica for twenty-five years.

For starters, we meet someone with a rage for community — a hunger for a family, possibly mythic, that will extend from a handful of comrades today to take in everyone on the planet next year. There's a Blakean exuberance in the openness with which Judy will encounter *anyone* warmly the first time. No matter how unprepossessing they seem, they're important; they have qualities and history, they might turn out to be part of the family.

Looking at the Rochdale stint, we can also discern her passion for justice, and her readiness to be the awkward one who first names injustice out loud. Along with her dauntingly unsentimental code of service. Anyone who truly needs her help will get it at once, in overflowing measure; anyone who merely wants it will likely get the brushoff — maybe civilly, maybe not. Life is too short.

But even that misses much of the point. What I really want to celebrate is the Judy who is inflamed by the dance of gestalts.

Let me sketch a scenario. Imagine a woman who is attracted to high energy levels, in any field whatsoever. And who's turned on by excellence of any kind. She gravitates to wherever those things can be found. And she has the knack of assessing a new field by quicksilver intuition — taking a depth scan, finding her feet almost instantly.

This is a woman who absorbs new paradigms like a sponge. That's what she's *about*. Details are okay, particulars are fine, but what really excites her is to discern the deep structure energizing them. We are talking about a woman who might go to Japan, and within days master the radically foreign syntax of that language — which *no* Westerner gets at first — drawn by the sheer sexiness of a new paradigm. (She might also remain unable to speak the language, never managing to persuade individual words to stick in her head.)

Now let's take two steps further. First, suppose the forms she's drawn to are seldom the ones other people tell her are there. (Though if they prove to be, that's okay.) For the one thing that compels her is the pattern that actually emerges when she wheels her own nervous system into place, sets it up, and waits. Waits for the irrefutable signal to go off: *here* is the shape of coherence, *this* is the living form.

From the outside, it may appear that in one of these whirlwind sessions she has simply absorbed a whole field at one slurp, and created a new synthesis. Which is not untrue. But what that leaves out is the galvanic rush the synthesis triggers. The new paradigm is not something *she* makes up. It announces itself, irrefutably, with the self-certifying little tingle of firsthandedness. And it's in precisely this buzz that the ecstasy of form resides — form as it crests on your nerve ends. Perhaps that's the only mode of worship open to this unlikely platonist . . . Anyway: given the possibility of experiencing gestalt highs, how could anyone be content to recycle shopworn models of order? That's a kind of self-denial she has no capacity for.

The second step is this. Imagine that our hypothetical woman is sometimes given access to a further level of formal eros. It occurs when she is permitted to observe, not just the pattern that energizes particulars in a single field, but something one level higher again: the way two patterns, or three, or many, can be active at the same time. In a single field, or across several at once — flickering in and out of each other, colliding, interchanging. It is a waltz of paradigms she is sometimes privileged to witness, a Siva-dance of gestalts.

It's so intoxicating she can't stay away.

It's obvious that I've been conjuring Judy Merril. And what I invite you to ponder is the way the scenario applies to each of her main endeavours. It happens to have come from watching her in action at Rochdale, where she could field all those cacophonous visions while others were just getting migraines.

Which is why she *belonged* there, the right resource person at the right time. But isn't it equally Judy the writer, spinning and twirling alternative forms of order before our eyes? And the Judy whose anthologies revolutionized the way we read speculative fiction? The editor who discerned new models in the cluster of paradigms which SF comprises?

To me, this is both the rarest and the most immediate thing to cherish in Judy Merril. She's a master of the eros of forms . . . Though each of us has our own Judy, and that's as it should be. We can never get enough of who she is.

Memories of Miron

Miron. Mirons. The memories now a jumble: the man more luminous than ever.

*

I remember one late-night session, at a party in Montreal. Was it in the seventies? We were goofing around, and on the spur of the moment we played a duet. I want to recall the moment as a triumph: the language of music transcending boundaries, language, isms. But in fact, it was a disaster.

Gaston played mouth harp, in a rough-hewn rural style he carried off well. For my part, I attacked the piano in an idiom composed equally of boogie, blues, and armageddon, somewhat tempered by my inability to play in any key but C major. Along with a tendency to stretch, shrink, or dispense entirely with the twelve-bar-blues form in which we were improvising. It took us about five minutes to clear the room, and another ten to realize we couldn't stand the racket ourselves. So we slunk back to the scotch, sheepish comrades in cacophony.

*

For the Gaston Miron of public record, I have to turn to reference books. Born in 1928, sixty miles north of Montreal — a country boy. Came to Montreal at nineteen, and did pickup jobs while he started to write. Cofounded l'Hexagone, a press which under his direction became the major poetry publisher in Quebec. A socialist, and passionately for Quebec independence from the beginning.

And then the poetry. Miron published exactly one full-dress collection, *L'homme rapaillé*, in 1970. Yet on its strength he came to be recognized as the godfather of postwar Quebec poetry, and received awards and honours throughout the French-speaking world.

And now the final entry. December 1996: dead of cancer.

★

My first Miron appeared when I needed him most.

I was thirty-one. Two years previously, I'd published *Civil Elegies* — meditations on the checkmate called English Canada. My dear, detested homeland: perpetual colony, which had never found the courage to exist as a public space. But then I'd lapsed into a dry spell. And I was paralyzed still; I was no longer satisfied with the *Elegies*, but everything else I tried was ringing false.

It was in this state that I opened *Ellipse* magazine, in the fall of 1970, at my home in Toronto. I could scarcely believe what I found. It featured translations from a poet called Gaston Miron. And I found myself reading lines like these:

> je n'ai jamais voyagé
> vers autre pays que toi mon pays

and these:

> je te salue, silence
>
> je ne suis plus revenu pour revenir
> je suis arrivé à ce qui commence

There was also an essay by Georges-André Vachon, who spoke of Miron's search for the poetry of his native space. "The poetry of his native space" — that was what *I* was after!

Who *was* this man? And what was he doing inside my nervous system? In English Canada, with the mammoth exception of Al Purdy, nobody wrote on public themes. Or if

they did, it was with the greeting-card quaintness of the
Maple Leaf school, or else a stentorian patriotism that made
me cringe. But to accept that words themselves are cankered
with our colonial nonbelonging; to recreate that dispossession
right in the poetic line; to wait on political resistance and the
word, in silence, to envoice our communal being — this was
a kind of heroism I had given up hope of discovering in anyone
with the same passport as me. But Miron was palpably the
real thing.

For months I fed on that poetry and essay. There was a
catalyzing affinity, as if with an older brother I hadn't known
was there. Eleven years my senior: a confirming presence in
Montreal. And while I don't suggest a direct cause and effect,
two years later the dry spell had ended. A revised version of
Civil Elegies came out, which was much more at home in its
skin. And anyone who reads the Miron issue of *Ellipse* will
know how profoundly I imbibed him. He helped me to claim
more deeply the words of *my* native space.

★

Another Miron. A snippet.

I'm sitting at a table, in a tiny square in Paris. One evening
in the eighties. And a woman I've just met is explaining to me
that *quality doesn't count*. She is in charge of implementing
gender policy at some Canadian cultural agency, I forget
which one. She wants none of my chauvinist bullshit about
good writing being better than bad writing; she wants 50%
parity in grants, with no reference to quality till that is
achieved.

I am a fellow-travelling feminist, three thousand miles from
home, and I'm thoroughly depressed. Why do good principles
always get screwed up? . . . At which point, my eye lights on
a poster across the square. Holy shit — it's Miron! Big square
mug gazing out at us. He was honoured in Paris last week; it's
an ad for a reading he gave.

In three leaps I'm across the square, prying the poster loose
from the brick. I lug it back to the table with an exaggerated

sense of relief. The conversation has taken another turn by now, but the icon will accompany me back to T.O.

Quality counts.

*

Around 1972, Miron came bounding up to Sheila Fischman at some do in Montreal. Apparently quoting an anthology that included four lines (four lines?) from *Civil Elegies*. Had Sheila ever heard of a guy called Lee? What about commissioning a translation for l'Hexagone? Sheila was gracious about the poem, and told Gaston of a partial version in French done by Marc Lebel at the University of Sherbrooke. And so that chapter of things began.

But what a large, pure, perfect gesture! Miron gets a buzz of recognition, reading four lines in a language he says he doesn't understand — and out he marches, to usher the whole works into French.

Once there were men like this. Right in our own time and place.

*

There is also the poignancy of Miron's own writing project. It shushes me.

A poet intuits a crucial space of words which has not been filled. The national epic of his homeland — which will tell its un-speakable truths, and in the telling help to itch that home-land into existence.

He can block in some chunks of the national epic. But unless he compromises the integrity of the colonized words which are his vocation and beloved, that's all he can do. Block in chunks. It is his failure, and also his triumph, that he will do no more.

Moses Miron.

*

I remember the first time I met Miron. In the spring of 1977, I had come to Montreal for a reading; Sheila Fischman picked me up afterwards and we drove to the Carré St. Louis.

I was nervous as all get out. Marc Lebel's translation was moving ahead, but Gaston and I still hadn't met. Now he would learn the truth. I really was a WASP, my French was spotty, I couldn't pass a test on the semiotics of Quebec poetry — all the liberal guilt in Toronto was churning through my system. I was Bay Street in blue jeans, the Plains of Abraham were about to come down on my head. Should I say "vous"?

What's odd is how little I remember of the meeting itself. Though perhaps it's not so odd. Because my main recollection is of the man's surpassing warmth, his sheer generosity of being. Along with that animal gusto! He took pains to greet me with "tu." I relaxed a bit. Then, still in the first minute or two, he sprang to his feet and declaimed some lines from the *Elegies.* In English first:

> Many were born in Canada, and living unlived lives they died
> of course but died truncated, stunted, never at
> home in native space and not yet
> citizens of a human body of kind . . .

Then in Marc's French:

> Plusieurs sont nés au Canada, et au terme de vies invécues
>   moururent
> bien sûr mais moururent tronqués, rabougris, jamais chez
> eux dans l'espace natal et toujours pas
> citoyens d'un corps d'espèce humaine . . .

I grinned, and relaxed some more . . . And that was that. We must have babbled for hours. What did we talk about? Who knows? I hope I conveyed a fraction of what it had meant to read his stuff. And like hundreds of others who encountered Gaston, I came away knowing I was special. I'd been met, understood.

★

There's one thing I never said out loud. Gaston had started the "Collection en tous lieux," to open the door to poetry from outside Quebec. And though much was opaque to me, I could see what a radical step it was to choose as an early title a book from English Canada. Openness to the world was one thing — but openness to Canada? It must have been playing with fire, even for someone as unassailable as Miron.

I wanted to tell him I honoured his courage. But doing so would have cheapened it somehow, crossed a line improperly. I was still a member of the erstwhile dominant culture, even if Gaston never treated me that way. And he wasn't breaking the taboo for the sake of earning my approval.

The only way I could find to salute that immense integrity was to take it at face value, and shut up . . . Heigh-ho: the subterranean communication of males. Did Gaston ever know how much I admired his nobility?

★

In 1979, Miron and Lebel and I drove to a house somewhere north of Montreal. Was it out in the country? We were going to spend the weekend doing a final polish of the translation. And what a marathon it was. We barely slept.

It would be my most intimate time with Gaston. Everything else fell away; we were up to our elbows in words. Our mutual master. But what the process revealed was how different our experience of words actually was. What a poet does in French, I began to realize, is profoundly unlike what a poet does in English. Even allowing for the individual differences on each side, their fundamental experience of language is not the same. Or at least we discovered a gulf of that kind, and in the end we couldn't bridge it.

We sat at a big table in the dining room, books and drafts spread out, and worked through the translation line by line. Marc was not a poet himself, and Gaston had many improvements to suggest: tactfully, but firmly. His grasp of the poem's content was glorious — far better than many anglophones'. I was at home in the discussion, though as usual beyond my depth when it came to nuances of French.

But we kept getting stuck. It was mostly with turns of phrase where I'd bent the English, played words off each other in an improvisational way that was strange even to English speakers, but that got something said I couldn't articulate any other way. And all I could steer by, for validation of the music, was that tiny, irrefutable *ping!* that goes off, sometimes on the hundredth draft, when words finally click into place.

After a lot of back-and-forthing, Marc had done his best to recreate this linguistic new-mintedness in French. But now, to my consternation, Gaston kept blocking the attempts. I wish I could cite some examples, but the drafts are long gone. All I have is the memory of Gaston reaching for his big *Robert* dictionary, yet again, with grave, implacable courtesy, to see if the vapour trail of nuance which Lebel was trying to bring across from English was listed among the seventeen meanings of the French word he'd chosen. If the twelfth entry included the connotation he was reaching for, the word stayed in. If not, it was toast. But as for re-imagining what language itself could do: there was no place for that.

I sat there flummoxed. What did this have to do with poetry?

I got a crash course in poetics that weekend — in French and in English. I found myself parading around the room, delivering fireball manifestoes I never knew I espoused (especially in the Alice-in-Wonderland French they emerged in). Okay, I declared: taken individually, I couldn't judge how the attempts to recreate my unexpected English were working. I didn't know how many of them emitted that unmistakable *ping!* in French. But taking the poem as a whole, you couldn't just standardize the language, plane it down, make it correct. (Jeez: did this sound like a defence of bad grammar? sloppy diction?) The English wasn't "correct"! It bounced through a dozen vocal registers, from slang to metaphysics, playing their musics against each other. You had cello, you had sax, you had kazoo. (I was hitting my stride now.) The poem wasn't just about its own content — it was a chancy trek through language itself. And sometimes, though barely, an arrival at the language of my unknown home. (Yes! The wild WASP in flight!) The reason its noises were so unfamiliar was that I was just learning to write Canadian. But if I followed words for real, I had to let them take me any-vocal-where they wanted; there was no safety net. (Go! Go!) And to screen out that dimension of verbal play was to geld the voices I'd been claimed by — which turned me into an obedient little Englishman, one more American. (. . . Yikes: this was getting out of hand. Did I really think Gaston Miron was a Yankee imperialist?)

There was a good deal more, which I won't go into here. The genius of English poetry since the Renaissance, I declared, has drawn on a language perpetually in process, made new, getting born and reborn in the instant the words hit the page. To tap into that process of "jail-break and re-creation," as Margaret Avison puts it, is to join a line of descent which includes Shakespeare, Milton, Whitman, Hopkins, Yeats. And which now includes whatever we do in the colonies, as we emerge into *our* unknown voices. If we can manage to be struck by lightning . . .

Gaston listened to all of this, with that huge innate courtesy, and went back to correcting Marc's French.

★

I was ready to weep with frustration and baffled love. And for the rest of the weekend, I couldn't fathom what was going on. All I knew was that the deep affinity which Miron and Lee had discovered was no longer there; at least not when we reached the heart of what claimed us both — the ache and resonance of words. Here, we were on totally different wavelengths.

Eighteen years later, I can see more of the picture. I know that "Miron" doesn't equal all poets in French; I shouldn't generalize just from him. I can also conjecture that his resistance to unconventional usage was of a piece with his refusal of joual. And that prompts a larger question. The point is not just what Miron was against (joual, harum-scarum linguistic innovation), but what he was *for*.

His relation to language was profoundly conservative. And so was mine. But what we were conserving was altogether different. When Gaston turned to his *Robert* for guidance, he wasn't being a fussy reactionary. He was reaching back into a living tradition, probing to see if these johnny-come-lately turns of phrase might legitimately extend it. I may never be fully at home with what that tradition finds sacred: a penetration to essence, a purity of expression which knows about the contingent, but doesn't wallow in it. (Have I said this without caricature?) Yet I *am* at home with intimations of the sacred, and with language as its vehicle. And with the knowledge that you don't play facile games with any of that.

For my part, when I assumed that English was up for grabs each time I sat down with a blank piece of paper, and that its very nature was to enact both flux *and* essence, I too was honouring the tradition I was born in. I was being equally conservative. But the integrity of each tradition was its own; the genius of one was not the genius of the other.

And neither could I assume that I was a special case. Miron's relation to language was not something to plea-bargain with. Even if he loved the poem; even if he cared for me. The craggy integrity that led him to publish *Civil Elegies* when he might be trashed for doing so was the same integrity that now insisted on good French. His life project was of a piece. I accepted both, or I accepted neither . . . Of course, I accepted both.

So there we were: three men in a room in Quebec, doing our level best at a quixotic project for no reason except that it was worth doing. And we were going to fail. There were realities our goodwill and mutual respect could not conjure out of existence.

At the functional level, we got the job done. Late Sunday evening, we drove back to Montreal. And the translation appeared in 1980.

★

I have a few more Mirons in memory. The book was launched at a reading with Gaston and Paul Chamberland — was this in Quebec City? — and we were back in synch again. We had a ball. And later in the eighties, we sat down together a few more times in Montreal. There was a palpable under-sadness in Gaston now, but the courtesy was still unfailing. And that uncanny mix of *spoudaios*, high seriousness, with sheer verve of being: that still prevailed. He gave me a copy of *Courtepointes*, inscribed — have I got it right? my copy isn't here — "Ces deux nations, nous les créerons ensemble." Fraternal independence.

I loved this man. And what I come to finally, if you'll allow me, is a poem I wrote two years ago. I never thought it would stand as goodbye to Miron.

Night Song

> Tell the ones you love, you
>   love them;
>   tell them now.
> For the day is coming, and also the night will come,
> when you will neither say it, nor hear it, nor care.
>   Tell the ones you love.
> I have lost many who mattered, and I will say it again:
>   tell the ones you love, you love them.
>   Tell them today.

Grant's Impasse

Beholdenness and the Silence of Reason

George Grant once gave me a particular gift. We were at his home in Dundas, near Hamilton, and I had been telling him about the place on earth where I most belong: a couple of acres on a lake north of Toronto, where I spent the summers as a boy.

"How *marvellous*, Dennis!" he boomed, with that outsize gusto which always took me off guard. A scatter of cigarette ashes came snaking down his cardigan. "How *marvellous*! It's what Plato said, isn't it?" Abruptly, I felt as if I was padding along ten steps behind in the conversation. How had Plato gotten into this?

But on he went — more gingerly, I thought. ". . . That we're meant to love the good." *What?* I tried to interpret the shift in his tone, since the meaning was still opaque. He seemed concerned not to offend me; apparently the connection between my childhood cottage and the good was so obvious, I might feel patronized if he spelled it out. ". . . And we come to love the good by first loving our own. How *marvellous* for you, having that place in Muskoka to love." More ashes tumbled onto the cardigan.

By loving our own! I still remember the little click as that phrase slid into place, and I realized I actually knew what he was talking about. Grant was giving me back my love for those pines, that rocky shoreline, the ramshackle cottage — giving it back in a luminous further dimension. For it was true: this was not just a casual attachment. To be claimed by that boyhood place of the heart, so deeply it almost hurt — that was inseparable from who I was. And it made sense. It was right. Loving our own is what human beings *do*. At the same time, giving my heart to that little patch of ground was something to grow ahead from. It had schooled me in the homing of desire, prepared me to love less immediate forms of (all right) "the good."

These were things I already knew, in a deep preverbal way. I just never knew I knew them. Not till I heard them spoken out loud in George and Sheila's living room. I've never forgotten the gift.

1. *Thinking Beholdenness*

One thing that spoke to me in Grant's work was his attempt to articulate something which could scarcely be thought at all within modern assumptions: that is, the reality of being beholden. It was a quest he pursued all his life, in fields as diverse as philosophy, history, art, political thought. But it was more than the private concern of one man.

In the modern era, we do not have rational categories which allow us to speak of being unprovisionally claimed, beyond all bargain or convenience: of being beholden by the very nature of things. We may or may not believe that anything claims us in such a way. But regardless of what we believe, this limitation is built into the grammar of modern thought itself. Its categories have been shaped to parse a world of objective facts and subjective values. And if there is a truth which can't be accommodated within those specifications, it will remain un-thinkable within the terms of modern rationality.

Over the last few centuries, very great thinkers have addressed this issue. Some I have read, like Nietzsche and Heidegger; others I haven't, like Kant and Hegel. But you start with what you're given. And for me, it was Grant's exploration of the question that clarified much of its shape and meaning. When I discovered his essays in the later 1960s, they confirmed hunches I was trying to field myself. Mind you, my search for a grammar of awe was going on in poetry, not philosophy, and its cast was often different from Grant's. But his driven, passionate quest was a landmark to steer by. I want to explore its substance here.

If you measure Grant's quest by the goals which he himself set for thought, I believe you have to judge it a failure. But that would be to miss the basic point. As far as I can tell, the goals he proposed were not achievable in the first place. Yet what he accomplished had a depth and resonance — a grandeur, I'd like to say — which make it exemplary.

*

A word about terminology. Grant believed that we are indeed beholden, and considered that recalling us to that reality was the primary task for thinking. But traditional terms for what claims us had either changed their meaning or been ruled out of court entirely. To make a start, he needed some interim way to name what he was pointing to.

His solution was to gesture with the language of classical philosophy: to resort to words like justice, the good, the eternal. In tracking his quest, I'll make use of these terms as well. They are not words I'm at home with, at least not on this grand a scale. (When I speak of being "beholden," I'm using a word I feel more comfortable with.) But I recognize that Grant was not promoting specific doctrines when he turned to this language. He was trying to rediscover what it would mean to think in a spirit of awe.

*

Grant came to the experience of beholdenness early. In 1941, he served as an air-raid precautions warden during the London Blitz. He was twenty-three. And a short time after, working on a farm in the south of England, he underwent a conversion which was unmistakably religious, though not sectarian. Years later he would describe it this way:

I just remember going off to work one morning and I remember walking through a gate; I got off my bicycle and walked through a gate, and I believed in God. I can't tell you more . . . I think it was a kind of affirmation that beyond time and space there is order . . . for me it was an affirmation about what is, an affirmation that ultimately there is order. And that is what one means by God, isn't it? That ultimately the world is not a maniacal chaos — I think that's what the affirmation was.[1]

This apprehension of ultimate order stood everything Grant had assumed until then on its head. The coherence of what is — this was not something created or measured by human beings. It was the other way round. Human beings were measured and judged *by* that coherence. It informed the constancy of the physical world, and the moral order which humans could sometimes sense. And its unconditional sway, which prevailed "beyond time and space," had already claimed us. "If I try to put it into words, I would say it was the recognition that I am not my own."[2]

The import of his conversion lay in this seismic shift. Human beings are beholden to the eternal; no other truth about the world could be as important. And with that, Grant's vocation was set. He would spend the rest of his life trying to make sense of the contemporary world, in light of the all-embracing order which sustained it.

In doing so, he would be seeking to articulate a reality which contradicted almost everything modern thought was equipped to say. That meant he would have to find different categories in which to think than those of modernity. And this would become the underlying theme of his work: the quest for a grammar of thought which could articulate beholdenness.

★

Over the next few years, Grant's conversion ripened into a Christian commitment. But he was uncomfortable with many aspects of Western Christianity, and he did not rely on theological categories in his mature work. What he was reaching for was philosophy — but philosophy of a kind that did not exist in the modern era.

He found what he was looking for when he began to read Plato seriously in the 1950s. Here was an approach which did not depend on theological doctrine, yet started from a recognition of the good, and interpreted human affairs in relation to its claim. Some of what he cherished in Plato can be seen in the account of natural law in his first book:

> The doctrine was the following: There is an order in the universe that human reason can discover and according to which the human will must act so that it can attune itself to the universal harmony . . . The truth of natural law is that man lives within an order that he did not make and to which he must subordinate his actions. (PMA, 27, 70)[3]

Grant was drawn to the doctrine of natural law because it articulated what he himself had experienced. But it couldn't be tabled as the self-evident truth about the nature of things. It could be appropriated only as part of an intricate shadow dance — always glimpsed from within the modern account of the world, which was based on denying it. Or more recently, on ignoring it entirely.

Broadly speaking, the modern account began its ascendancy in the West after 1600, particularly among the educated. According to it we live in an objective universe, governed by laws we can discover. And we understand it most rigorously through what came to be known, after Galileo and Newton, as the scientific method.

The new science described a universe of neutral phenomena, devoid of intrinsic meaning. Over the centuries, its prodigious success appeared to confirm the validity of this model. And moral and political thinkers helped to reinforce its status, by dissolving the classical belief that human affairs should be interpreted in relation to the eternal. Finally, within this "value-free" universe — so runs the authorized version of the last hundred years — we create history and meaning by acting on our subjective values.

Over the last four centuries, then, such categories as "nature," "thing," "cause" have been progressively redefined — specifically to exclude whatever traces of non-empirical meaning still lingered. Thus any attempt to speak rationally of what "the eternal" once meant has been shut down before it begins. We can no longer think about such a thing with intellectual probity in the first place; we have canonized categories of thought which render it meaningless.

But while Grant recognized the enormous achievements of modernity, and celebrated its alleviation of physical suffering and want, he resisted its stance in this regard. He could not surrender the ancient truth: that we are claimed by an order which is not subject to our will or convenience. Had he not experienced that claim firsthand? Yet it was all but impossible to see how it could be thought coherently within the modern paradigm.

This set Grant's theoretical goal for philosophy. We cannot deny the efficacy of modern thought; we cannot surrender the truth of ancient thought; we must find some way of "thinking them together." (PMA, 70.) But while he proposed that goal as the desideratum, his own deepest thinking would take a very different direction.

*

"Concerning the more difficult and more important theoretical questions, my debt is above all to the writings of Leo Strauss."[4] Grant paid this tribute in 1966 to the thinker, twenty years his senior, who had laboured to re-establish political philosophy on a classical foundation. For about five years after 1960, Strauss's account of modernity had a profound impact on Grant — confirming his previous insights, and raising high hopes for philosophy. His eventual parting with Strauss would be a turning point in his quest.

Grant found in the older man's work a sweeping yet detailed account of political thought since Machiavelli. Strauss interpreted the modern tradition as a conscious rejection of natural law, and a series of attempts to find an alternative. By what principles should we now conduct our public lives? What all modern thinkers had in common, though they sometimes fudged the fact, was that in their accounts, "Justice no longer consists in complying with standards that are independent of human will." (*NRH*, 187.)

With Rousseau, political thinkers had turned to history as the source of guidance. "For a moment — the moment lasted longer than a century — it seemed possible to seek the standard of human action in the historical process." (*NRH*, 274.) The historicist approach reached its climax in Hegel and Marx. But the moment couldn't hold:

> The historical school had succeeded in discrediting universal or abstract principles; it had thought that historical studies would reveal particular or concrete standards. Yet the unbiased historian had to confess his inability to derive any norms from history . . . No objective criterion henceforth allowed the distinction between good and bad choices. Historicism culminated in nihilism. (*NRH*, 17–18)

This was a literal nihilism: there was nothing to steer by. And Strauss uncovered a second strain in modern nihilism as well. As science systematized more and more of the world, it had seemed that separating subjective values from objective facts would preserve a space for goodness/beauty/truth. But when those grand ideals are denied participation in a sacred and claiming order, indeed are denied any reality beyond an arbitrary subjectivity, they lose all their cogency. "Once we realize that the principles of our actions have no other support than our blind choice, we really do not believe in them any more. We cannot wholeheartedly act upon them any more." (*NRH*, 6.) Thus the fact/value distinction led to the same dead-end as historicism. From 1600 to 1900, the nihilism latent in modern thought had worked its way to the surface.

But there was more to be found in Strauss, for he didn't simply anatomize modern thought. He declared that its central assumptions collapse under scrutiny, and that classical thought gave a truer account of things.

As long as he stayed on the offensive, Strauss's arguments were telling. But things got dicier when he tried to show the superiority of the ancient account. For he wrote as if, in stating the classical view, he had already restored it to life; as if he had somehow escaped from modern assumptions, without having to account for their unparalleled success — which was based on a denial of ancient truth. Or such was Grant's objection. He would have loved to go along with Strauss; but where was the concrete, reasoned account of the primacy of the eternal, stated in terms one could accept today?

Grant explored his qualms in 1964, at the end of "Tyranny and Wisdom." After a respectful account of Strauss's arguments concerning ancient and modern tyranny, he was forced to report that they did not deliver the goods. Grant's profound disappointment comes through all the more for being understated:

> To ask the question, by what criteria the rulers of the good and wise city were to make these determinations . . . would, I presume, draw from Strauss the reply: by that virtue and piety which are described in the leading classical books on moral and political philosophy. The issue then returns to the completeness, adequacy and concreteness of that teaching. Strauss's position would be easier to understand if he would explicate the classical teaching on this matter. (*TE*, 101)

Grant found the same disturbing reticence — he refrained from calling it "evasiveness" — when it came to the other great tributary of modern thought, that of Judaism and Christianity:

> I can only state that Strauss's writing shows a remarkable reticence whenever he writes of Biblical religion . . . Since Strauss is attempting the remarkable and prodigious task of restoring

classical social science, how can he maintain his reticence at this point? (*TE*, 108–9)

★

For all his tact, Grant was now parting company with Strauss on grounds of intellectual honesty. But it was not a step he welcomed. For if classical affirmations could no longer be appropriated, then his own goal — of thinking ancient and modern truth together — was also at risk. His faith in the eternal had not abated. But how was he to articulate it?

And the problem went far beyond one man's perplexity. For if there is any sense in which we are claimed by a reality other than ourselves, then a civilization which denies that fact, indeed proscribes all rational categories which permit it to stand as a question, has done itself incalculable harm. All its deepest wisdom, except for what value-free analysis can mediate, has been set beyond the limits of the thinkable. And the effect on how that civilization conducts its affairs — not just in philosophy, but across the board — will be catastrophic.

It was this dilemma which Grant would address in the late 1960s, in the essays of *Technology and Empire*.

2. *Grant's Impasse (I): Technology*

As Grant's reliance on Strauss diminished during the mid-sixties, he had begun to engage with Nietzsche, Jacques Ellul, and Heidegger. It may have been reading the latter that provoked the dramatic coalescence in his thinking which now ensued. From the present perspective, three of these meditations stand at the heart of Grant's achievement: "The University Curriculum," "In Defence of North America," and "A Platitude."

Following Heidegger, Grant would now take "technology" as the most suitable name for the stage which Western civilization has reached. The term referred to two things at once: the

external phenomena which the word usually denotes —
machines and inventions and specific techniques; and simultaneously, the stance of mind and will of the society which
brought those things into being. Now he could speak in
one breath about the external and internal realities of our
civilization:

> Technique is ourselves. All descriptions or definitions of tech-
> nique which place it outside ourselves hide from us what it is . . .
> Technique comes forth from and is sustained in our vision of
> ourselves as creative freedom, making ourselves, and conquering
> the chances of an indifferent world. (*TE*, 137)

And this gave him a new purchase on issues that preoccupied him. It meant he could situate modern forms of
imperialism, progress in science and technology, the doctrine
of radical freedom — in fact, a multitude of contemporary
phenomena — within a common matrix. Its character was
this. In the technological world, nature is taken to be not
merely neutral, but raw material for our use; and "nature"
includes not just trees and lakes, but other peoples, outer
space, our own bodies. So too our past, our knowledge, our
"values" comprise a stockpile for use and profit. Everything
exists to be processed by human will, using instrumental
reason and technique. In fact, we don't just use technique; we
are it. Technology is our fundamental way of being in the
world. It is our ontology, and by its nature it excludes rational
access to all modes of being but itself.

So far, Grant was recapitulating Heidegger and Ellul. But at
this point he took a decisive step of his own. His intent all
along had been to analyze the astonishing civilization which
surrounds us, and to show how it grows from the modern
stance toward the eternal. That is where he had been stymied
in the past, because he could not find an acceptable way to
think the eternal from within modernity. But now he stopped
treating that difficulty as an obstacle to be sidestepped or dealt
with later. Instead he took it as the central subject of thought.

To put it differently: perhaps Strauss's failure to give contemporary substance to classical truth was not due to his strategy of reticence. Perhaps he was unable to say what knowledge of the good would consist of today — *because it couldn't be said*. And perhaps the only step possible was to analyze that condition of rational muteness. Perhaps thought was called, not to think from outside modern nihilism, but to think the impossibility of doing so: to anatomize its own impotence toward meaning.

I've come to think of the dilemma he was addressing as "Grant's impasse." This was not a personal difficulty which Grant blundered into when he tried to think about justice or the sacred (though he could not avoid thinking within the bind). Rather, it is a systemic checkmate in our civilization — an independent condition of thought and life. It was there before Grant wrote about it; it would have been there if he had never lived. Thus the usage is parallel to "Pike's peak," "Halley's comet," "Gödel's theorem."

★

In broad terms, Grant was addressing the problem of modern nihilism. As we've seen, this derived from the fact that our version of reason has nothing to orient itself by except its own dynamic. It has posited that the external world is value-free; this leads to the conclusion that traditional "values" are relative, arbitrary, in fact value-free themselves. A host of difficulties follow, which thinkers since Kant have addressed.

But given that familiar picture, Grant was not just recycling the litany of modern angst. He was asking a particular, targeted question — one which focused the issues in a novel way. It was not a question about nihilism *per se*, but rather about our attempts to escape it. And it might have seemed unnecessary to ask, had our attempts to date not been such unrelieved failures.

The question was this: what happens when modern reason tries to criticize its own condition? If technical thought reaches for something beyond itself, something qualitatively different from its own assumptions and techniques, what can it achieve? The question was crucial for Grant, since his goal was to articulate the claim of the eternal. But it applied to all thought in the technological era, whenever it tried to address something other than itself. To put it simply: was there an escape clause in modern thought?

Grant's answer was this. Any critical thought about technology is bound to reproduce that technology — right in the assumptions and methods of the thinking itself. The attempt will reenact the condition it is trying to judge. We may long to escape the nihilism we're enmeshed in. But we cannot think our way out of it, because we can't stop recreating it in the very texture of our thinking.

A good deal of Grant's energy in the late sixties was spent getting this insight into words. As far as I can think his findings through, he uncovered two stages of checkmate. His concern was to give true testimony, however, not to create a detailed taxonomy of mind ruptures. So in distinguishing these two stages, I will be supplying a more explicit shape to his analysis than he himself proposed.

There was a lot of bad news in these essays, but there was other news as well. And to do Grant's thinking justice, I should present both kinds at once. But I'll have to separate them artificially here. I'll start with the bad news.

3. *Grant's Impasse (II): Judging Particular Techniques*

The first stage of the impasse occurs when we attempt to "judge particular techniques." Grant described this stage as follows:

> The difficulty then of those who seek substantive values by which to judge particular techniques is that they must generally think of such values within the massive assumptions of modern thought. Indeed even to think "values" at all is to be within such assumptions. But the goal of modern moral striving — the building of free and equal human beings — leads inevitably back

to a trust in the expansion of that very technology we are attempting to judge . . . As moderns we have no standards by which to judge particular techniques, except standards welling up with our faith in technical expansion. (*TE*, 34)

The difficulty begins when we try to judge a particular example of the technological project — the technique of mass production, say, or that of cloning animals. And to do so, we turn to some idea or value in our inherited repertoire of critical thought and moral judgement. But we discover, on looking closer, that this outside arbiter is no longer accessible as such. When we ponder the substantive value on which we want to base our judgement, we can't avoid perceiving it as an historically determined belief, a function of class and ethnicity, or whatever. That is, our understanding of its status collapses back into the same assumptions about the world that underlie the technique we're trying to judge. And when this happens often enough, the whole project of thinking critically or judging morally begins to founder.

Grant appears to have identified this self-reflexive circle most clearly in 1967, while writing "The University Curriculum." The particular technique he considered there was fundamental: the method of "non-evaluative analysis" (*TE*, 124) which now prevails, in varying forms, as the paradigm of knowing throughout that curriculum.

The tight circle in which we live is this: our present forms of existence have sapped the ability to think about standards of excellence, and yet at the same time have imposed on us a standard in terms of which the human good is monolithically asserted. Thus, the university curriculum, by the very studies it incorporates, guarantees that there should be no serious criticism of itself or of the society it is shaped to serve. We are unable seriously to judge the university without judging its essence, the curriculum; but since we are educated in terms of that curriculum it is guaranteed that most of us will judge it as good. (*TE*, 131)

This was the only concrete example of the impasse Grant would provide in *Technology and Empire*. To bring the argument further down to earth, we have to turn to examples from later books.

★

One of the most elegant is found in the lustrous late essay, "Thinking About Technology." It takes as its point of departure the reassurance, by an unnamed computer scientist, that computers need not be feared. They are under human control; it is up to us to use them for good or malign purposes. The reassurance runs, "The computer does not impose on us the ways it should be used." (*TJ*, 19.)

Grant situates that pronouncement within a reiteration of the impasse:

> The ways that computers have been and will be used cannot be detached from modern conceptions of justice, and these conceptions of justice come forth from the very account of reasoning which led to the building of computers. (*TJ*, 27)

Grant then examines more closely what is contained in the second part of the statement. The crux is the word "should." In the course of a prolonged analysis, he unravels the speaker's apparent desire to have things both ways: to embrace the assumptions of value-free technology, and also to speak the language of moral imperatives — even though the latter have been ruled out of court during the development of that technology:

> "The computer does not impose on us the ways it *should* be used" asserts the essence of the modern view, which is that human ability freely determines what happens. It then puts that freedom in the service of the very "should" which that same modern novelty has made provisional. The resolute mastery to which we are summoned in "does not impose" is the very source of difficulty in apprehending goodness as "should." Therefore, the

"should" in the statement has only a masquerading resonance in the actions we are summoned to concerning computers. It is a word carried over from the past to be used in a present which is ours only because the assumptions of that past were criticised out of public existence. (*TJ*, 31)

And at that point, the speaker's reassurance dissolves. Within the assumptions of his statement — which are those of our civilization at large — there is finally no content to "should" beyond a further application of technology:

When we are deliberating in any practical situation our judgement acts rather like a mirror, which throws back the very metaphysic of the technology which we are supposed to be deliberating about in detail. The outcome is almost inevitably a decision for further technological development. (*TJ*, 33)

And those who wish to challenge this process, to suggest that we have lost sight of something more basic than the effectiveness of a given technique, find themselves tongue-tied:

Any possible long range intimations of deprival of human good cannot be expressed in the ontology they share with their opponents . . . But there is no other language available which does not seem to be the irrational refusal of the truths of scientific discovery. (*TJ*, 33)

Thus the attempt to judge the "particular technique" of computers has led to a dead-end.

4. *Grant's Impasse (III): Intimations of Deprival*

The next stage of the impasse is no longer concerned with the dilemmas which surface when we try to think about particular techniques. That is, the thinker is no longer moving from "problem" to "critical/ethical solution" to "collapse of that solution," finding that each new solution turns out to re-embody the problem.

Instead, he tries to break directly out of the impasse: to think an other-than-technological reality which he senses himself deprived of — and discovers that he has skidded into white space, unthinkability, ground zero. If reason short-circuited in the first stage, it is here lobotomized. For in this second stage we find we can no longer *name* — not in the world of public discourse, predictably enough; but scarcely even to ourselves — the thing we lack.

Grant explored this second stage most profoundly in "A Platitude." His account turned on the "intimations of deprival" which haunt the denizen of technopolis:

> All coherent languages beyond those which serve the drive to unlimited freedom through technique have been broken up in the coming to be of what we are. Therefore it is impossible to articulate publicly any suggestion of loss, and perhaps even more frightening, almost impossible to articulate it to ourselves. We have been left with no words which cleave together and summon out of uncertainty the good of which we may sense the dispossession. (TE, 139)

> All languages of good except the language of the drive to freedom have disintegrated, so it is just to pass some antique wind to speak of goods that belong to man as man. (TE, 141)

In this second stage of the impasse, then, the mind is foraging for categories simply to name the realities which modern thought has ruled inadmissible. And the search engenders an all-but-withering despair, for it appears that we cannot find any such categories unchanged by modernity. Yet if we cannot think those things in the ways we know *how* to think — how can we think them at all? We are necessarily mute as rational beings, even in the privacy of our best intuitions. At this point, the nihilism of the modern project seems complete.

★

As we will see in the next section, Grant did not just come to rest in this despair. But before we proceed, we should take stock of what he had accomplished.

Twenty-five years earlier, he had set out to give rational witness to the claim of the eternal, and to interpret the world in its light. But what he achieved in *Technology and Empire*, almost against his will, was something very different. He had anatomized an endgame of reason in which there was no possibility of construing either "claim" or "eternal" as non-provisional realities. That is, he had declared (among other things) the impossibility of giving the rational witness to which he was called. This was such an unexpected outcome that it takes some getting used to. As a trial perspective, let me set down some observations:

Grant's vocation was intellectual contemplation — and in *Technology and Empire*, that is what he achieved. But (to repeat) what he found himself contemplating was virtually the opposite of what he hoped to find. Nonetheless, this was a faithful eros of knowing, in which the fate of our era achieved some of its true contemporary names.

What he uncovered did not prove the truth or falsity of the faith he had held since his conversion: that we are claimed by an eternal order. But it showed that within the modern paradigm there was no way to interpret the world rationally on the basis of that faith. It was not that better attempts were needed; no attempt would work. For someone whose calling was philosophy, this was bitter medicine.

Grant was not simply analyzing the difficulty of proclaiming his own faith. He had uncovered a strange loop in our condition. And if his analysis was accurate, as I believe it to be, then every attempt to escape the limitations of modern thought in the ways he described will be subject to Grant's impasse. That is: anyone who sets out to judge particular techniques within the horizon of modern thought, or to articulate realities which technology cannot recognize, will find the attempt short-circuiting.

This is thought at the foundation level: thought about the

necessities imposed by thinking itself. And it effects a short but crucial step in the self-knowledge of modern nihilism — which is to say, in the world we inhabit and are.

This is not a vocation any sane person would choose: given the closing down of articulable meaning in our civilization, to chart the inability of modern reason to break the deadlock. But the closing down was already a fact, and somebody had to think the impasse. One person to whom the task fell was George Grant.

The cruel question was this: what could you possibly think next?

*

Grant's own self-assessment was that he was not a philosopher of stature, and possibly not a philosopher at all. And while this judgement was extreme, there was something to it. His singular gift was for penetrating to questions that matter, and engaging them at the deepest level. But he always began by pondering how thinkers he considered his betters had approached those questions; and this he did with agonizing care, sometimes for decades. Perhaps because of that prolonged expense of concentration, perhaps because of his own limitations, his work did not open up new and original directions for thinking, nor find unprecedented ways to think. It simply burrowed more and more profoundly into the place it began in. This inability to find a new starting ground for thought is at least part of what he intended, I believe, by his unsparing self-assessment.

It would be proper to reply that Grant had no desire to be original. But the fact remains that he identified the unification of ancient and modern truth as the *sine qua non*. And finding how to think them together would have been a feat of the greatest originality. Faced with this task, he reported that it was beyond him. My own assessment, then, would be that Grant did indeed enter the arena in which philosophy is accomplished; but that he made little positive progress. Of course that already separates him from most of us who claim to think independently, or who teach philosophy.

Yet even if this is true, it ignores the most important fact. For a spell in the late 1960s, Grant's gifts as a seeking thinker came into phase with a dilemma of thought which demanded to be articulated. It may be that thinkers before him had identified this quandary in late modern thought, and parsed it with equal cogency. Certainly Nietzsche, Heidegger, and Simone Weil wrote with consummate insight in this area; Grant stood in awe of their achievements. But while it may simply reflect the limitations of my reading, I don't know any passage in their work which gives such a detailed account of the way modern reason, when it tries to judge or escape its situation, recreates that situation by the act of thinking itself.

But that is a question of historical fact, which people more informed than myself can adjudicate. What I do know is that Grant's exploration of the impasse had a life-on-the-line urgency, a largeness of spirit which conveyed the sense of first and last things. What he achieved may have been precious little. But that is what it was: a precious little.

5. *Grant's Impasse (IV): Intimations of Good*

Decoding the impasse didn't mean that Grant had escaped it himself. His faith was still rationally mute. But neither did it change the fact that he had been claimed by the eternal. Even if he could not articulate that claiming within modern categories, and even if he had found no other categories to think in, his vocation of witnessing remained in force. He had good news to declare.

We must now go back and consider something we did not bring into view above. That is, the way Grant kept lacing his analysis with reminders that we are nudged, claimed, inflamed by the good. This was essentially a joyous affirmation, even if he seemed at times to make it through clenched teeth. For it was true: justice and the good had been darkened in the modern era. Yet they could never be extinguished. And experiencing even glints and hints of their reality was at least as primal a given as was the impasse itself.

The first step was modest enough. Grant insisted that, however tight the vise of technological civilization, it was incumbent on us to work at the practical level to achieve good ends — or at least to limit evil ones. Thus he declared, at the end of "Canadian Fate and Imperialism":

> Nothing here written implies that the increasingly difficult job of preserving what is left of Canadian sovereignty is not worth the efforts of practical men. (TE, 77)

The job was worth the effort because a Canada which retained even a hobbled independence might resist the murderous purposes of empire. And in general, Grant insisted that the bleakness of what he was reporting did not imply that we should abandon any good fight, however limited its chance of success.

★

But this wasn't all. Grant kept reminding the reader of occasions which point to a different reality from anything technology knows of:

> The fact begins to appear through the modernity which has denied it: human excellence cannot be appropriated by those who think of it as sustained simply in the human will, but only by those who have glimpsed that it is sustained by all that is. Although that sustainment cannot be adequately thought by us because of the fragmentation and complexity of our historical inheritance, this is still no reason not to open ourselves to all those occasions in which the reality of that sustaining makes itself present to us. (TE, 133)

When he evoked such occasions from his own experience, the results were moving. One passage celebrates the intimations which his time in Oxford had brought. He speaks of

things more deeply in the stuff of everyday living which remain
long after they can no longer be thought: public and private
virtues having their point beyond what can in any sense be called
socially useful; commitments to love and to friendship which lie
rooted in a realm outside the calculable; a partaking in the
beautiful not seen as the product of human creativity; amuse-
ments and ecstasies not seen as the enemies of reason. (*TE*, 36)

Most of us know such occasions. The sheer ache and delight
in a son or daughter's life, which leaves us knowing we're
committed for keeps, beneath all calculation and convenience. The way a place corrals us — a patch of Muskoka, a
hallowed childhood spot in the back lane. The central *yes*
of confirmation when we witness an act of pure integrity,
be it public or private. That irrefutable arc of desire, let
loose by a piece of music. The shudder of recognition when
a movement of thought rings true, even though it dis-
lodges convictions we'd hoped to cling to. Who among us
has not encountered things we can neither bargain with nor
disown? Things to which we are beholden? Things for which,
in our best moments, we would go to the wall? This is a
knowing that unfolds in a different dimension from anything
we hear of in the modern account. And if we are unable to
think such knowledge rationally, that does not invalidate what
we know.

Grant strove to bring this kind of knowing — these bittersweet intimations of good — back to the centre of our attention.
For even though he couldn't say how to think their meaning,
they were a lifeline.

Any intimations of authentic deprival are precious, because they
are the ways through which intimations of good, unthinkable
in the public terms, may yet appear to us . . . The language of
good is not then a dead language, but one that must, even in its
present disintegration, be re-collected, even as we publicly let
our freedom become ever more increasingly the pure will to
will. (*TE*, 141–42)

The positive side of Grant's achievement lay in identifying our intimations of deprival as the itch, the necessary irritant, for future thought about the good.

There were other ways in which he tried to bring us to this recognition. Sometimes he forced the reader through an almost unbearable exercise, contemplating what technological thought implied at its most extreme.

One telling example came when he spoke of categorical limits.[5] Is there anything in the modern account which recognizes that there are things we must never do? And the answer is no. Within that account, even to ask such a question shows intellectual bad taste. Modern knowledge can tell us about the value systems of different societies. But by its own assumptions it is obliged to treat them as neutral data, and concentrate on analyzing their structure and dynamics. It specifically excludes the notion that any value might be true; that an action might simply *be* evil, for instance. An action can no more be evil, in the modern paradigm, than it can be rectangular or plaid.

But if we bring that account face to face with certain extreme examples, it appears daft. Consider the kind of limiting case which clarifies the whole landscape: a sadist who rapes and tortures two-year-olds. Anyone who is not a moral cretin knows this behaviour is evil. And if a social scientist explains that their certainty may be "true," but only in the context of their particular value system, they will shake their head and walk off. In a case like this, our sense of a categorical limit is not negotiable. People should never torture children. Period. And if modern thought does not permit us to speak of unconditional evil in such a case, there is something lacking in modern thought itself.

★

Grant found further ways of recalling us to the good. Sometimes he pointed to what ancestral memory, enshrined in tradition, can tell us. And his prose itself was a kind of holy prod; the long, unfolding cadences of grief and desire became a form of incitement, evoking a way of knowing which had nothing to do with technological thought.

This is the basic fact about *Technology and Empire*: it both anatomized Grant's impasse, and strove to remind the reader of another way of knowing and being. It could not rise to a rational enactment of that way, and hence it could not articulate the thing it sought to awaken us to. But it incited its readers to persevere, to honour the best they knew. They might or might not have been granted the religious promise, that in doing so they were cooperating with the eternal itself. But in either case, their intimations of good were the truest thing they had to steer by.

And this double stance revealed the deepest meaning of the impasse: that the desolation it produced was the mark of our fittedness for good. To believe there *was* no impasse — that would be worst of all: to live in hell and not know it. It would mean we had reneged on our glimpses of saving knowledge: that goodness is real, that evil is real, that the claim of truth upon our lives is real. And so to face into the impasse with radical clarity, to parse it in a thinking which glowed with celebratory rage and grief, was itself a way of loving the thing we cannot think. Beyond that, if Grant could not give rational witness to the eternal, he would continue his witness outside the bounds of modern rationality.

6. *Openings*

Much more could be said about this. How Grant approached the impasse in later books. How he treasured elements of modernity, such as political freedom, despite his hatred of modern assumptions. How he tried to influence public life in light of the good, even though he couldn't articulate its claim in the language of modern public life.

But it's time to take a different tack. When I ponder Grant's thought today, I find it both exemplary and limited. The reasons I love it will be evident by now — starting with his craggy demand that we recognize what matters, regardless of its thinkability. But what about the limitations of his thought?

I'm constrained in speaking about this, since I'm not a philosopher. For me, the way the world makes sense is not primarily conceptual; the coherence of things comes through as a cadence of being, a cosmophony. So if I comment on these matters analytically I do so as an outsider, in a language not my native tongue.

That said, I can't help wondering whether the theoretical goal Grant set for philosophy was the only one possible, or the best one, or even one that defines our aspirations helpfully at all. Consider a passage like the following, from *English-Speaking Justice*. He speaks of the need to hold classical thought and modern science together: to think their truths "in unity." And then as always, he declares the task impossible:

> The darkness [which has fallen upon justice in modern times] is fearful, because what is at stake is whether anything is good. In the pretechnological era, the central western account of justice clarified the claim that justice is what we are fitted for . . . Why the darkness which enshrouds justice is so dense — even for those who think that what is given in *The Republic* concerning good stands forth as true — is because that truth cannot be thought in unity with what is given in modern science . . . In the darkness one should not return as if the discoveries of modern science had not taken place; nor should one give up the question of what it means to say that justice is what we are fitted for; and yet who has been able to think the two together? (*ESJ*, 87–88)

But is it so clear that our only option is to think classical truth and modern science in unity? Defining the goal of thought this way may help to ensure that we stay trapped within the impasse.

And I also wonder this. When Grant posed the issue in these terms — as he would continue to do till the end of his life — did he recognize the implications of what he had already accomplished in *Technology and Empire*?

That achievement amounted to a negative demonstration of the first order. By way of analogy, I think of the Michelson-Morley experiment of 1887. It had set out to verify the effects of the hypothetical "ether," which had been posited as the universal medium of transmission for light. But considered in those terms, the experiment was a failure. Not because it was inept, but because it proved impossible to detect any sign that the ether existed at all. As a result, the hypothesis had to be scrapped — which threw classical physics into disarray. Yet within twenty years, Einstein had resolved the quandaries which this created by reconceiving the fundamental nature of space and time.

In some respects, Grant's analysis of the impasse was analogous to the Michelson-Morley experiment. His initial aim had been to show that the truth of religion was consistent with modern science, as people had argued for hundreds of years. But what he ended up showing was that the rational framework in which the attempts were being made guaranteed, in advance, that none would succeed. Moreover, the impasse applied not only to traditional forms of piety, but to any attempt to arrive at a secular ethic within modern assumptions. The checkmate was total.

Given that demonstration, I have difficulty understanding why Grant went on pursuing the very goal — the unification of ancient and modern truths — which he had shown to be impossible. Yet this would continue to define the framework of his quest right up to his last major essay, "Faith and the Multiversity."

But surely his analysis pointed in an entirely different direction: that is, to the necessity of reconceiving modern thought itself. Of finding new categories to think in. As Einstein (to return to the analogy) would do with the basic grammar of physics.

    *

Let me pursue this line of conjecture before I query Grant's approach further. How realistic is it to speak of "reconceiving modern thought"? My hunch is that it is not only realistic, but mandatory.

If you step back from the modern account of the world, it seems bizarre that it hypnotized us for so long. I'm not thinking now of particular scientific theories. I mean the dualist model which non-scientists devised in order to account for the efficacy of those theories. They pictured a universe composed of neutral bodies in space, on the one hand, and consciousness on the other: a world of objective facts and subjective values. For centuries, this account was taken to be self-evidently true (in its successive versions), however bleak it appeared. But unless I'm missing the point, no such conclusion about its status was justified.

To say that we need a better account has nothing to do with disputing the truth of scientific theories, however. It's a matter of challenging a model which interpreted those truths naively.

*

The world can be successfully represented by an array of equations. It is a property of what exists to be scrutable to mathematical science.

Nor does this scrutability obtain solely in mathematical disciplines. Modern scientists have devised closed, a-valuative systems of explanation for studying everything from evolution to public opinion to the human brain. They have objectified everything under the sun, and beyond it. And when those systems are tested, the phenomena they deal with behave in ways that can be accounted for within the systems. (If they don't, of course, a better system must be sought.) To repeat: the world is scrutable to scientific knowing, even though that knowing is highly abstract and reductive. But this leads to a further question: what does this scrutability *signify* about the world? There are various interpretations possible, and it's not immediately obvious which we should adopt.

I can't pretend to a detailed knowledge of the stages by which the modern worldview came to maturity. But one thing is clear: thinkers assumed increasingly that the universe we live in is identical with the universe described in the equations of Galileo, Newton, and their successors. Among possible ways of interpreting the scrutability of what is, this naive realism was the most simpleminded. It took for granted that the world has the same character as the equations which model its behaviour. If the equations are quantitative and value-neutral, the world must be too.

This momentous assumption was never proven, needless to say. It's not even clear that the thinkers who adopted it considered it to *be* an assumption; it may have appeared self-evident. In any case, over the centuries it gave rise to the great hypotheses of the modern paradigm: the split between objective matter and subjective consciousness; the fact/value distinction (which was effectively grafted onto the first); and as a concomitant, the historical relativity of truth.

But the status of that assumption was altogether different from the status of Galileo and Newton's equations. The equations were mathematically impregnable; the model of a universe of facts and values was a speculative hypothesis — and an extremely unsophisticated one at that. Yet because the equations were so potent, the men who devised the model were able to drape it in Newton's mantle: to present it as being, no less than the laws of thermodynamics, the scientific truth about the world.

The model cannot be validated by reference to the truth of scientific theory, however. What the modern thinkers were actually faced with was the following state of affairs. If we create a body of knowledge which posits that the objects of its knowing are value-free, that knowledge will tell us about the behaviour of value-free objects. That's what it was designed to do; that is all it *can* do. But this is tautological. In retrospect, it seems bizarre to have been so dismayed when it refused to do anything else.

If we put a blue filter on a lens, we see a blue world. And if we put a value-free filter on the lens, we see a value-free world. The analogy is imperfect, mind you, because it doesn't allow for the aspect of prediction and verification. When we use a mathematical filter, it can sometimes specify in advance how the world will behave. That is, we aren't just projecting blue onto things that are not-blue; we're discerning a blueness that is already there. The filter resonates with, locks into something deeply engrained in how the world goes about being itself. And whether or not we use the language of mathematics, there is nothing extant which can't be productively analyzed as neutral and value-free.

Yet recognizing that remarkable fact, and admiring it, and wondering that it should be so, are very different from concluding that the filter *is* the world. That is intellectual naiveté. What we need is a much more sophisticated way of understanding the scrutability of what is to objective analysis.

★

It is time to undrape the modern account. To strip it of Newton's mantle.

The dirty secret is this: the worldview of facts and values is on its deathbed. It was naive to begin with, and there are realities which it cannot accommodate. We can walk off and let it expire without prolonging the old, defensive debates.

We are free — no, we are obliged — to think the world in terms which are inadmissible within modernity. To do so publicly, soberly, ecstatically, and as often as possible.

What would a more adequate account look like? How *should* we picture what is?

I don't have a concrete answer, and it would trivialize the question to propose one here. There are thinkers of stature who have devoted their lives to this enquiry; I hope to keep learning from them. But when I ask what a more sophisticated account would consist of, I find myself with questions of three kinds.

1) Wouldn't such an account have to provide a framework in which more than one order of truth about the world applied simultaneously?

I don't mean the bifurcated way we understand that notion now — where the hard truth of facts obtains in the external world, and the sentimental truth of values is given free rein in subjective consciousness. Surely we need a still-undiscovered form of relativity, where everything that is — external world and consciousness alike — exists in the order of necessity, and can be analyzed across the board as structured and value-free; and at the same time, everything exists in the order of good and evil, beholdenness, the categorical claim of truth. The world is factual; the world is meaningful; both truths are true. This was Simone Weil's intuition, though it's not clear (to me at least) how far she was able to translate it into concrete thought before her death.

The only form of reason worthy of the name would then be one which could move responsibly among two or more dimensions of polyphasic truth. I presume this would call for new rational categories, new forms of analysis, new canons of rigour. Perhaps it would include some way of thinking a connection between the dimensions. And certainly there would be no excuse for admitting wishful thinking or hare-brained notions as "true." That's what we encourage now, when we exile questions of meaning to the chimerical realm of subjectivity.

2) The order of scientific truth will look after itself. But if we had a more sophisticated rational framework in which to think — as we do not, at present — how should we proceed in the order of truth where value-free knowing does not provide the protocols? When we think about the world using categories of meaning, what exactly *would* we think?

Here too I do not have a concrete model to propose. But I recognize one of Grant's intuitions as pivotal. That is: we would do well to begin, not from general doctrines or theories, but from our experience of non-provisory claiming in the everyday world. We should look to "things more deeply in the stuff of everyday living which remain long after they can no longer be thought." (*TE*, 36.) And at the outset, we would not need any grander categories than that in which to inter-pret them. All we would need is a passion to identify things by which we know ourselves, experientially, to be claimed.

Eventually those primals, those normative nodes, would come to *constitute* our basic categories. The goal would be to configure our account of the world-as-meaningful around them. I might add that I wish Grant had spent more time telling us about the things that claimed him. He wrote about them superbly, but far too seldom.

My own primals include the following: the recognition — sometimes reluctant — that truth has a deeper claim upon me than do my own inclinations; the certainty of categorical moral limits — otherwise put, the recognition that evil is real; the (sporadic) accuracy of intuitive leadings, which I know as a matter of course from writing; the way I began by loving my own, and then widened the circle of loving; the hard brick wall of awe; the knowledge of being beholden — sometimes with no object to attach it to. And I'm not surprised by the fact that other people have different primals, nor that their recognition of moral limits is prompted by different occasions. We may differ about how to describe a chair; that doesn't mean the chair isn't there. What matters first is that our primals should emerge from concrete experience. After that, we can struggle to find a grammar of thought in which to think what they imply about the world.

3) This brings me back to Grant's classicism. Once we accept the bankruptcy of the modern account, it seems to me, we are not automatically compelled to return to ancient accounts, nor to labour at reconciling classical truths with science. We have another option: we can start from what we know in the here and now. And insisting that our only choice is to derive our rational categories from Plato, or from any other classical source, may finally shore up the tattered hegemony of the modern, when we discover time and again that we cannot accomplish the task.

Moreover, some of our primals are likely to come with a freight of older beliefs and doctrines attached. And if we are committed in advance to "restating classical truths in contemporary form," we will be unable to think clearly what we know for ourselves about those primals. Our minds will be clouded by the need to find modern formulations for God, the good, the soul, providence, life after death, etc. But that has nothing to do with thinking openly and rigorously in the world we inhabit.

Once we step outside the claustrophobic absurdities of modernity, and open ourselves responsibly to what compels us, we will have done the best we can. We can only trust that the truth of what is true will find us; how that relates to the truth the ancients were given is not under our control. We can check our discoveries against those older verities, as one does when there are respected elders present. But the final authority lies in what we know experientially to be the case.

*

I remember my sense of exhilaration, thirty years ago, when George Grant became my mentor. Before we met; before he even knew I existed. And then, across wide differences and silences, my friend. I still remember that floodtide gift of himself.

Old comrade, beached exemplar, great spirit: I do remember. I hope we learn from you well.

Notes

1 Grant never wrote about his conversion, but he began to speak about it in interviews when he was nearly sixty. This description comes from David Cayley, ed., *George Grant in Conversation* (Toronto: Anansi, 1995), 48–49. The interview took place in 1985.

2 Larry Schmidt, ed., *George Grant in Process: Essays and Conversations* (Toronto: Anansi, 1978), 63. The interview took place in 1977.

3 Grant (1918–88) published six books: (1) *Philosophy in the Mass Age* (Toronto: University of Toronto Press, 1995; first published in 1959; cited as PMA). (2) *Lament for a Nation* (Toronto: McClelland & Stewart, 1965). (3) *Technology and Empire* (Toronto: Anansi, 1969; cited as TE). (4) *Time as History* (Toronto: CBC Learning Systems, 1971; delivered on the CBC in 1969). (5) *English-Speaking Justice* (Sackville: Mount Allison University, 1974; cited as ESJ). (6) *Technology and Justice* (Toronto: Anansi, 1986; cited as TJ). In quoting Grant, I have silently supplied capitals at the beginning of quotations, and omitted words like "that" when they are anomalous within an excerpt. The meaning is never affected.

4 PMA, 122. The tribute occurs in Grant's introduction to the 1966 edition. The conservative political philosopher Leo Strauss (1899–1973) was a German Jew by birth, an American by adoption. Of his many books, I've drawn on the four to which Grant himself refers: *Natural Right and History* (Chicago: University of Chicago Press, 1953; cited as NRH); *Thoughts on Machiavelli* (Chicago: University of Chicago Press, 1958); *What Is Political Philosophy?* (Chicago: University of Chicago Press, 1988; first published in 1959); and *On Tyranny* (Ithaca: University of Cornell Press, 1968; first published in 1963).

5 Grant first pursued this line of thought in PMA, 84–89. His own preferred example of the categorically wrong was judicial condemnation of the innocent. He returned to the subject in ESJ, and in "Nietzsche and the Ancients" in TJ, where he argued that modern liberalism has no rational resources by which to judge genocide as evil.

PART THREE

The Luminous Tumult

[From an interview conducted by Donna Bennett and Russell Brown in August 1993]

Dennis, you published an interim version of Riffs *eleven years ago, and the finished sequence has just appeared. That's a pretty long gestation even for you. I'm interested in what you were wrestling with.*

During most of that time, I couldn't see what the structure of the sequence should be. Actually, I didn't know what *kind* of a sequence it should be.

Can you talk about that? I mean the concrete issues of craft? For instance, you'd already written two long poems, Civil Elegies *and* The Death of Harold Ladoo. *Were they any help?*

Oh no. Apart from the business of orchestrating different voices, they were no help at all. Almost the opposite.

So how did Riffs *begin?*

With a kind of vocal meltdown.

Meaning —?

It was only the second time in my life that a new voice has come out of the blue. It happened with *Civil Elegies*. And it happened again with this much jazzier voice, in the spring of '81. About a thousand of these little pieces came through in a couple of months.

My personal life was pretty fraught at the time, that was part of it. I was living in Edinburgh on the Canada-Scotland

163

exchange — away from distractions here, so I had high hopes for writing. But I wasted months on a long poem that was terrible, I wrote the polyphony essay, and that was that. And my marriage broke up at Christmas. I was sitting up every night in the flat, drinking and picking scabs.

And then in May, these *things* began. I remember the first night. I had the headphones on, playing some Buddy Holly, and I started doing a kind of automatic writing. About a love affair I'd gotten into, which was on hold because the woman had gone away. It came in quick little stings; I'd scribble down one, draw a line, start the next. And the voice kept jumping around, all these honks and bleats and weird unofficial music. It was just noodling, though. I had no idea I was starting *Riffs*.

Anyway, I got up the next morning and found thirty-five of them. Most of them were just therapeutic garbage, but a couple had a funny quality I didn't recognize — one of them started:

> Home-spooked
> hotline.   Nobody's li'l number
>
> one.   Big-eyed
> radium child on stretched-out scrims of alert . . .

Now, something like that coming out of your pen can get your attention. It sure got mine. Here I was, a meditative poet who did long, ruminative, publicly resonant things — I had a perfectly decent way of writing already. What was *this* about? But the next night I tried again, and along with the crud I got a few more with that bizarre crackle and pop.

Still about the love affair?

Still about the love affair — or the lack of it. So it became the thing I *did* at night. Pretty soon there were hundreds and hundreds of them, in this whole marching band of voices. They could sound like this:

> Wal, acey deucey
>   trey divide —

I'm a guy
    with a fine wide-eyed

lady freckles too &
    squirms when she
feels good . . .

Or like this:

Am going soon, but meanwhile I can hear
what mortals care for,
instep and desire.
Tell me what you cherish, won't
just walk; give me lifetime,
not renege . . .

Or this:

Blood on
    behemoth.

Tracts of sheer
    unness.

Abyss and
    interludes.
I did that thing, I just can't walk home straight.

And on and on it went, night after night. With the voices going all over the map. And you've got to understand, in the late seventies I'd been writing one or two short poems a year — none of them remotely like this.

Who else was writing this way? "Unofficial music," you called it. In these little blurts, with the influence from jazz and rock and blues, and with literary decorum out the window. It seems like a very North American mode.

It is. But I hadn't seen a whole lot of it even here. This kind of music — it's not the same thing as the conversational voice you hear in so much of North American poetry. It can draw on vernacular and slang, but it's really about the process of vocal improvisation itself; that, and the pulse of feeling. It's a riffy, iffy, intuitive thing. Individual pieces are often light-weight in content, but the music itself makes the real declaration. So the music is what you read for first of all. If I had a parallel life, I'd spend a month doing an anthology: "Songs from the Wrong Side of Town," something like that.

Who would be in it?

I'd look for pieces that trace out a coherent arc of feeling — that really *are* songs on the page, not just yea-many lines of improv. One centre of gravity would be Berryman's *Dream Songs*. Line by line they have this fractured musical torque: all those virtuoso stomps and hollers, mating calls to whatever. Like that little blues:

> I'm scared a lonely. Never see my son,
> easy be not to see anyone,
> combers out to sea
> know they're goin somewhere but not me.
> Got a little poison, got a little gun,
> I'm scared a lonely . . .

That may sound easy to do. But if you think it actually is, look at something like Auden's "Refugee Blues":

> Say this city has ten million souls,
> Some are living in mansions, some are living in holes:
> Yet there's no place for us, my dear, yet there's no place
> for us . . .
>
> Went to a committee; they offered me a chair;
> Asked me politely to return next year:
> But where shall we go to-day, my dear, but where shall
> we go to-day? . . .

Auden never got it at all, he was only slumming. But Berryman keeps pulling it off again and again, this wonky music.

Who else?

Well, you'd have some early cummings — from those sex

sonnets, say, where he was clearly working from jazz. Kerouac, if there's anything in *Mexico City Blues* that still stands up. Definitely some Creeley. Like "Jack's Blues," with that nifty last stanza:

> I'm going to roll up
> a rug and smoke it, put
> the car in the garage and I'm
> gone, like a sad old candle.

Maybe Don McKay, though what he does with that amazing vocal flair is a bit different. You'd want the one by Paulette Jiles that starts:

> Honey, you know when you talk like that
> you're the only man I'll ever love.
> Just keep talking.
> That's what you're good for . . .

And the one by Lorna Crozier that ends:

> Hey, big talker,
> waited all my life
> for a man like you.
> Come my way, I'll blow
> the fuses in your big machine,
> short all your circuits . . .

So we've got a possible anthology underway. But meanwhile, what did you do about Riffs? *It's now the spring of '81, and you've written a thousand of them.*

Well, by summer the affair was over, and I was back in Toronto. And the run was finished too; it had lasted three months. There were maybe a hundred pieces I could see working with. It got as far as the version that appeared in *Descant* in 1982, but it still wasn't right. And the passes I made in the next few years didn't get it much further.

So it's been a two-stage process. First, the arrival in this chariots-of-fire fashion, with a rough shaping. And then ten more years, while I tried to figure out what I had on my hands. I wrote another five hundred pieces along the way, but I didn't get the whole thing right till last year. Once it fell into place, it was hard to see why it had taken so long.

Just to complete the picture: I started another sequence, "Nightwatch," in 1985. It's been my co-albatross along with *Riffs* — for a while I thought they were part of a single long poem. So for the last eight years, both sequences have been on the go.

Looking at the shape of Riffs, *I'm struck by the fact that it* is *a sequence, rather than a continuous long poem like* Ladoo. *The way you've described its evolution, that seems like the appropriate form for it to take. Could you talk about how you shaped it?*

The first thing is that it came in these little spurts of improvisation. Intense, close-up, with the emotional and linguistic experience tracked right on the page. They really are riffs, which by definition are quickies.

I presume people know what a riff is. The word comes from jazz, and it refers to one of those little melodic improvisations a soloist does. Though strange to say, back in the swing era a riff was what happened when the gentlemen in the brass section stood up and went, "Wah-WAAAH, wah; (Ta-dah, doo-dee-die); Wah-WAAAH, wah . . ." And then the soloist comes in, "Da-zingo, *snick!*; Zooom, gobble-da-gobble-da; Wacko doo-dah-*dit*; And the price of fish!" — all that in four seconds. And then the "Wah-WAAAH, wah" brigade starts up again. The latter being basically rhythmic, with no melodic interest and no particular feeling. And of course scored in advance, since everybody had to play the same thing . . . And in the thirties, that's what a riff was. But by the kind of transfer where "Frankenstein" went from being the mad scientist to the monster, "riff" went from being the rhythmic filler to the solo fireworks.

So these things came through as riffs. But that made the question of structuring them hard to deal with. Emotionally, the focal length was about a thousandth of an inch. The pieces have almost no distance on the experience they're about; at their riffiest, they aren't about an experience at all — they *are* the experience. Often there's no paraphrasable content. And that confused me. The fact that they relied on voice, that much I was at home with. But my adult stuff had always had heavy-duty content too, and these sure didn't. What on earth is the "content" of something like this?

> SKID skid, dopey li'l
> juggernaut;
> Molotov sidecar momma, wrench me a frog.

> If you got happiness tablets throw some out the window way
>   down opposite side.

There's just this feeling of revved-up emptiness, and the vamping in words.

If there wasn't much content to steer by, how did you organize them?

That was the big question. At first I hoped the vocal trajectory itself would tell the story. There weren't many themes — as in musical themes. Boy gets girl, feels good; boy loses girl, sucks thumb. That was about it. So I hoped you could take that for granted, and concentrate on the tonal changes; you'd hear the shifts from voice to voice tracing out the emotional progression — from goofy to sad to grave, and on and on. But it didn't work. After you'd read a couple of dozen of these things, you just went into a trance; there was no sense of forward movement at all.

Which made me question some of my ideas about polyphony (right after I'd written the essay about it, of course). Those first runs at *Riffs* were pretty uncompromising, the way they took shifts of voice as the only structural guide. It wasn't surprising that some people couldn't connect. The voices were weird. But even readers who liked the noises — myself, for a start — got bogged down. It seemed as if an extended sequence, at least when it was made up of so many short pieces, needed more than just a vocal trajectory to hold it together. Only with these things, what else *was* there?

What did you do?

I was stymied. I never thought of turning them into a continuous poem — with no section breaks, I mean — but I must have tried every other wrong-headed possibility. That first version in *Descant*, for instance. It had a narrative line of sorts, but I had to spell it out in prose at the beginning, which was pretty mechanical.

The problem was, I was trying to tell a story in a series of quick takes. And while each could give you a single, stop-time moment, that seemed to scotch the possibility of telling a continuous story. The speaker's wigged-out consciousness wasn't available for narration, that's for sure. Not credibly. But if you tried to shift into the third person — so you could move around, set the scene, all that — you undercut the speaking voice completely. If we're going to trust that voice, with its strung-out intensity, there can't be some other, more matter-of-fact intelligence stage-managing the thing. You can't have it both ways . . . Poe was the first to talk about this stuff. But he just said, go for the lyric intensity. A long poem, with all the paraphernalia you have to include, is a contradiction in terms. And that's where I was stuck. I wanted more than just a songbook, but I couldn't find a formal logic for the whole thing.

What about your interest in jazz? Did it give you any formal leads? . . . Let me frame that another way. Would you call yourself a jazz poet? In Riffs, *I mean?*

Not necessarily. I'd call it jazz poetry; it stands or falls by the sense of improvisation it gives. But whether or not the only way to get that is by literally improvising — which means using only first drafts — that's a separate question. A first draft may have exactly the right quicksilver moves, and I'm chuffed when it does. But if the fiftieth draft has more of that white-hot feeling, of the words coming into existence the second they hit the paper, that's the one I go with. The experience on the page is what counts; the way you achieve it is irrelevant. So I was always prepared to revise.

Language just isn't the same medium as pure rhythm and sound — you're dealing with meaning as well. And that makes it a different animal. Sometimes you have to inch your way toward improv in a poem.

But jazz has been important in your writing, hasn't it?

Jazz has been my biggest influence in the last decade. Even though it didn't kick in seriously till after that spring in Edinburgh, believe it or not. The improvisational leads I was following back then came from abstract expressionism, and some remarks of Charles Olson's.

Let me clarify this. I don't mean "jazz influence" the way you find in beat poetry, where you caught some live music and tried to recreate the way it felt — you went on about the searing purple of the orgasmic sax, and the writing itself was pretty purple. Those people may have loved jazz, but they didn't know enough about poetry. So I don't take jazz as the subject matter. Nor as a program you try to imitate in words. Occasionally in *Riffs* there are things that fool around with explicit musical references . . . you know, you'll hear a phrase from the blues, or a little run of polly-wolly-doodle. But that's just local kibitzing, it's not the kind of subterranean influence I'm talking about.

It's partly the improvised form that kills me in jazz: the way the melodic shape conjures itself out of nowhere. And also the exploration of pure feeling. In older recorded jazz they had two or three minutes to work in, and they moved so fast, into such an intensity of emotion. Straight to the blood-stream! Look at those solos by — oh, whoever: the sax is what speaks to me most, so Parker, Ben Webster, Lester Young. Small-group stuff before the LP, especially bop. There's a couple of lead-in bars and there you are, inside this pure ache or exultation as it finds its shape, flowering out of its own insides but also part of what the whole group is doing with some old sock of a theme — and then, wham! it's over. That kind of magic my body just feels at home in. It's had as much effect on my recent poetry as anything I read — often I miss that fireball grace in literature. But still, the affinity is with individual riffs; it didn't help with the shape of the whole sequence.

The music I hear in your poetry, particularly Riffs, *exists at the level of rhythm and syncopation. Something is going on in the line that's similar to jazz.*

It's partly the phrasing. In *Riffs* it comes in bites; sometimes there's a long arching line, but it always unfolds after a series of quick swoops. There's a sense of pounce, of staccato phrasing — I can talk about it better with body English than I can in words.

That prosody opened up while I was working on *Riffs*. Previously I'd gravitated to a long tumbling line. With a cross-tension set up by the line breaks, and by syntactic splaying within the sentences. But with *Riffs*, I started to hear a different kind of rhythm. To catch it, you need to feel the underlying energy, the cadence, muscling up through the words and propelling the piece ahead. It may be easier to hear if you set a couple of these rhythmic idioms side by side. It's the difference between how the energy moved in *Civil Elegies*, say:

> Often I sit in the sun and brooding over the city, always
> in airborne shapes among the pollution I hear them, returning;
> pouring across the square
> in fetid descent they darken the towers
> and the wind-swept place of meeting, and whenever
> the thick air clogs my breathing it teems with their presence . . .

And the way it moves in *Riffs*. For instance:

> Hey, should I
> talk
> sociology?
>
> *when where what how who?*
>
> All I

want, woman, is
crawl up your left nostril & snuff it for keeps in sexual asthma
   heaven.

You can feel the difference in the two kinds of locomotion,
right? And plugging into this edgier way of moving was part
of the electricity.

Was that connected with your sense of improvisaton?

Absolutely.

*But how can you sustain that with a poem you've worked on for
so long? . . . Trick question.*

But a good one, believe me. It would have been easy to lose
the spur-of-the-moment feel. Particularly because the pieces
I've written in the last couple of years, which coaxed this final
shape out of the sequence — a number of them are more
poems than riffs. And in a poem, you're working with a different kind of consciousness, more self-aware. The sequence
needed that, so I wasn't just shooting everything in close-up.
But finding how to move from riffs to poems to riffs again
without wrecking the fabric of the whole thing: that was crucial.
   Not everything in the book is a riff, in the sense I'm talking
about. Some of them, I don't know *what* they are, and maybe
they're the purest riffs. They were the scariest. But others are
recognizably poems. If you nailed me to the wall and said,
name the three characteristics that distinguish a riff from a
poem, I probably couldn't. But as the guy who wrote the
thing, I know there's a difference.

Was there any difference in the way you wrote them?

Definitely. The riffs began with a pell-mell first draft; the
poems came a few lines at a time, like my previous stuff. The
riffs were harder to do, because I had to disconnect my brain.
And when the full-tilt-boogie improv was happening, it felt
as if there was this whole flux of pre-meaning; there was a
groundswell of dangerous energy, and the words bubbled up
from that. The improvisation depended on walking into it,

and getting hit from all sides. Even though you might change the words later on.

If you just sit down and analyze a riff, you're likely to get this wrong. You can dissect the wordplay, say, the riffle-shuffle of meanings — and fair enough, that's part of the spoor of the energy. But you're starting from the wrong end, if you give "meaning" precedence over the luminous tumult it rises out of. *That's* what sweeps you along, not just the twiddles and hiccups of sense. If *Riffs* is erotic, it's because that energy is — not simply because some of the pieces talk about making love.

Along with explosions of individual riffs, the sequence explodes a personal relationship. Are those things related?

Well, yes and no. Let me talk about the personal element first. The pieces did begin in a real affair, and for several years I kept pretty close to what actually happened. But that was naive. It was only when I started listening to the affair on the page that I found my way ahead. And then it could go anywhere. So if you treat it as a documentary episode from the author's life, you miss the whole point. All that matters is the emotional truth it's exploring. Along with the music, of course.

But there's one real-life thing I didn't tamper with, and *Riffs* could hardly exist without it. The guy in the book has a whirligig romance, the woman goes away, and he starts these nightly sessions. But words are the only thing he's got now, so words are where the lightning has to strike. The riffs themselves become the erotic fix.

Now, that had been my own experience in 1981 — of engaging with "sheer valhalla overdrive" in words. And without my even realizing it, that became the central convention of *Riffs*. The guy making his nightly grab at glory, scratching the numinous itch. Over and over, till it becomes an addiction. Because one thing the sequence is doing is trying to improvise a connection with the sacred, when the old ways of connecting have been shut down.

But that creates a weird circularity. You know? Each riff is a finished object; but at the same time, it's a gesture. An action. A pass at one more high in words. The act of cruising for one more riff, that *is* the present-tense plot . . . Though with a certain brittleness, I'd say. This is electroshock loving, not the deep resilience of two lives over decades. And it's a large burden to lay on one little affair. In fact, on writing itself. It's a form of idolatry. That way burnout lies, and eventually the sequence has to mime the sound of his nervous system crashing . . . But my job was to track those things, not make the guy live more sensibly.

Anyway, that's a formal strategy I could never have arrived at by planning. It came straight out of the original experience. Even calling it a "strategy" seems a bit wrongheaded, since it was such a mix of lunacy and luck. But it supplies much of the underpinning for *Riffs* as a dramatic poem.

When you speak of it this way, I wonder why you felt it needed any further continuity. Beyond this improvisational quest by the speaker, what were you after?

You do these things in the dark. When I was dissatisfied all through the eighties, I couldn't say why it felt unfinished. It just did. I wanted something you'd read both ways: as a sequence in ecstatic form, *and* in linear form. But I couldn't see how to manage it . . . I remember rereading the *Dream Songs*, to see what Berryman had done. But even though I loved individual pieces, the sequence as a whole wasn't any help, because as a sequence it doesn't work. In the first instalment, Berryman had this tenuous hook he hoped would give it some coherence — the Henry/Mr. Bones routine. But that kind of peters out. And eventually the songs just accumulate, to the point that all 385 are a lesser whole than 30 or 40 of them. Going back to it confirmed my sense that a batch of bare naked riffs was always going to be just that. A batch. A miscellany. A sequence needed more linear purchase than he'd located, more forward momentum. Or equally to the point, more than I had.

I also went back to *Maud*, which I remembered as having
some killer lyrics *and* a story line. But the whole thing was
sandbagged by a different problem, which I hadn't solved in
Riffs either. It started whenever I tried to give my speaker a
daily life where things actually happened, which is one of the
approaches I experimented with. But how was he supposed
to trot out some brisk reportage on the day's events, considering the state he was in? And anyway, it wouldn't have
worked. I winced at the way the speaker in *Maud* narrates the
external plot, and his credibility flies out the window. All
you're aware of is Tennyson forcing the poor sod to recount
things to people who've just lived through them *with* him,
earlier the same day. It throws you right out of the poem . . .
And the problem goes deeper, too. The speaker in *Maud* is
wingy, and that's where the lyric energy comes from — like
in that uncanny piece where he imagines himself dead, with
feet tramping over his head. But the fact is, that voice doesn't
believe in linear time. The pure ecstatic moment, even if it's
pure despair, is the only place it's at home. So the plot poems
clank like Halloween skeletons. They're just not good poetry,
they come from Tennyson's superego. They're doing what Poe
criticized long poems for, wedging in structural stuff that puts
us to sleep . . . All of which was painfully evident in my own
drafts. Poe was wrong about *The Iliad*, but he was right about
those versions of *Riffs*.

But you still haven't told us what you did. *How you finally got
it to work.*

I won't go on about the rest of the things I tried; they could
stand as a survey of how to botch a lyric sequence. And the
move that finally took didn't involve a new formal principle
at all. It meant changing one detail — namely, making the
woman married. It seems absurd, but that brought the whole
sequence into synch with itself.

I'd always been bugged by the question, why don't these
two get back together? If the guy is missing her so much, why
doesn't he just go see her? (The autobiographical reason, that

their lives lay in different countries, was no use in the poem.) But once I gave her a husband, things fell into place.

At the simplest level, it explained the blockage in their affair. Now the woman could be away on a trip with the husband, trying to decide whether to stay with him, or leave him for the guy who's speaking. Plus, the story that sustained the riffs didn't have to describe a lot of new events. It could consist mainly of discovering that things we'd read near the beginning were not as we'd thought. It never *was* an innocent love affair. So you could have a backward-leaning, forward-tilting narrative — revelations about the past would propel the present ahead. This was hardly news in fiction, but it wasn't something I'd seen in lyric poetry. And I liked the formal effect. As you read, you could go mainly with the stop-time riffs; or you could let the emerging story define the shape; or you could do both.

And now the polyphony, the trajectory of voices, could enact the emotional flow. Once it wasn't being asked to carry the structural load all by itself. And so the deeper currents of feeling could start to animate the sequence. I haven't said much about them, but I imagine they're obvious: the hunger, the shame, the sense of sterner moral necessities, the cold-turkey withdrawal from this big emotional jag. It's a funny thing. You're working with an energy that isn't literally on the page, yet it has to breathe life into the whole poem. It's like trying to open a space for the wind to blow through. The words are just the track of its going, they're not the energy itself. I find this one of the most mysterious things in writing an extended poem. The most important thing you're working with is never literally there.

Did it do anything else, making the woman married?

Well, it seemed to resolve the problem of credibility when the narrator talked about events. It may be an unwelcome fact that somebody whose lover is married will deny her commitment — deny it to himself, first of all. But while that may be reprehensible, it doesn't strain our belief. So for the speaker not to mention a husband for half the sequence, then lurch into flagellating himself about it — that felt realistic.

And it went a step further. The speaker has had access to eros central; and we believe it, I hope, because of the accents of joy in his voice. But when it develops that it's all been triggered by a season of tacky adultery — what are we to make of *that*? I loved the artistic leverage it gave on quandaries of good and bad. It opened into uncomfortable mysteries I'm gripped by. And now I could explore them straight-on, without constantly tripping over technical difficulties that weren't germane.

I scarcely realized it at first, but making the woman married allowed a clean, invisible economy across the whole sequence. It made *Riffs* finishable. So with some help from my wife and friends, and the excellent editor at *Brick*, I finished it.

Poetry and Unknowing

*[From an interview conducted by Michael Higgins,
Peter Hinchcliffe, and John Porter in 1993]*

I

You've been called a philosophical poet. Is that accurate?

Some of the time, I guess. But more basically, I'm a meditative poet.

When I was starting to write, back in the sixties, I was very caught up in philosophical and critical thought. But I hadn't sorted out the difference between that kind of thinking and the meditative process. So my first book was logjammed with ideas, or at least with allusions to them. Maybe the poems were philosophical at one remove, if there's such a thing. But enacted meditations they weren't.

Part of the problem was technical. It boggles me now, but *Kingdom of Absence* was a sequence of sonnets. With some of them structured *as* sonnets, and others kind of bouncing off the form. But that was exactly the wrong way for me to be writing, in a tight, preset structure. The lope and sprawl and return that are intrinsic to meditation had no room to breathe, to stretch out and sniff around. Eventually I realized that writing a meditation involves — certainly the mind, but also the heart, the body, the spirit. It's a quest, a quest of attending, and it unfolds on all those wavelengths. That's what I had to learn to do on the page.

Which leads to voice, and the way that orchestrating voices can create a trajectory of meditation. I sometimes think I'm an idolater of voice. For me, to speak in shorthand, voice embodies being. A given voice can catch the texture of one particular way things are. And if it rings true, you sense it resonating with things on that wavelength across the whole breadth of what is. Which permits a kind of sonic mapping of the world.

What's more, a poem can be polyphonic; it can move from voice to voice. Poetic meditation isn't just a matter of going from content A to content B to content C. A meditative poem does its job when the vocal shifts themselves enact a trajectory — first embodying *this* content in *this* voice; then idling sideways to embody new content in another voice; then spurting ahead to a third inflection. Moving in the free-form way we do when we're tracking something that matters with our whole life. And that vocal trek itself constitutes a way of knowing.

What it comes to is this. Voice *embodies*; polyphony *enacts*. And if you're lucky, it enacts an ontophony, a music of being . . . Talking about ontology can be iffy, I've realized; the word alone seems to generate a smog of abstraction. But ontophony is less heady, less teuto-ineffable. On a good day, it just resonates in things. It's there to be heard.

You read philosophers like Grant and Heidegger. Do they help to shape the voice, or the voices, of a poem?

Not for me they don't. Philosophers can identify things to wrestle with: Heidegger and Grant, as you say, Simone Weil, certain others. And of course prior to that, daily living does. But the actual vocality of the wrestle — that doesn't come from any philosopher I read. It's the to-be-grappled-with, the to-be-meditated that generates the voice.

How do you know what it's supposed to sound like? You don't "know"; it's an intuitive process. And intuition is intriguing, because it means you're engaging with something that to all intents and purposes isn't there. If you knew what a given poem was trying to be, you could just write it down. But in this case you're responding to something you feel claimed by, but can't yet do in words. Or maybe even identify.

Athletes proceed that way at times. Wayne Gretzky watches himself on videotape, and he can't understand why he's suddenly zooming off-screen to the left. Then he realizes he was reacting to something that wouldn't happen for another five or six seconds. Which is a long time in hockey. Some hunch made him ghost to his left, with no obvious reason — except here comes the puck, and zap! It's in the net.

It's a funny business though. It would be nice to believe that your intuitions were always right. But anybody who works this way knows it just isn't so. Intuition can take you to wonderful, unexpected places; it can also land you in all kinds of dead-ends and goofy mistakes. And you're likely to get the same sense of an epiphany high, whichever it is. So it's like any other form of knowing — it has to be tested and confirmed.

You mentioned "polyphony," which is one of the key terms in your poetics. Another is "cadence." And you've spoken of how hard it is to define what that means.

I still get tongue-tied. "Cadence" is my name for the flux, the felt and living flux that poems rise out of. It's where the voices come from — it *is* the voices, intuited first without words. But when this polyphonic tumble is coming through, the sense I get is that I'm a function of it, rather than vice versa. Only how do you talk about that, when talking depends *on* it?

Not that talking about it is the point. Months or years can go by and I don't think once about "the nature of cadence." All I'm doing is trying to get some words right on the page. So when I'm working on a poem, my brain is empty of theory. It's full of plans, though; I always have *the* great structure in my head that's going to resolve everything. But that's never the way it works out. The actual advances have to do with local stuff. You know — why is there such a lurch on the middle of page three, when it moves from one section to the next? It doesn't work, and I keep coming back and worrying away at it, and eventually I realize that the second section doesn't belong in the poem at all. So out it goes. And then a month passes and I think, well, there's one little run in the cancelled chunk that might feel good if we segued into it over here — which is eleven pages further on. So I try it there . . . You know? You're trying to do justice to the way something wants to move. You don't know what the something is; you don't know what the shape of it is; you're just mucking about in the middle, trying to honour what feel like the lines of force.

This mucking about seems to involve a great deal of revision. How does it work? What happened while you were writing The Death of Harold Ladoo, *for instance?*

Well, it's both a typical case, and not. Harold was murdered in 1973, and for months afterwards I wanted to write something for him. And then one day some stuff started coming through. It was basically the lines that are italicized in the finished poem, which address Ladoo in this very elevated style. And it seemed that *was* the poem. I thought, "This is great, I'm finally paying my dues to Harold." I played with it that first day — there were about fifteen lines, which seemed almost enough — but when I came back the next day, it wasn't quite right. So I fiddled a bit; and a bit more . . . and away we went. It took a year and a half, and ended up maybe 750 lines long.

I found myself working with this funny process of kickback, of argumentation with the initial impulse to do a high-style elegy. It had never occurred to me that you could make a poem out of your quarrel with "Lycidas." But I began to realize there was a certain dishonesty in that first draft. There was nothing untrue in the praise of Ladoo, but it sure papered over a lot of complexities. And I didn't know what to do about that. Until I realized that my ambivalence should be enacted right on the page. So I started breaking taboos, exploring things that qualified and undercut and painted moustaches on the Mona Lisa of a nice lofty eulogy. The new stuff didn't even feel like poetry. But getting it onto the page, letting it break through in a series of jagged pendulum swings, each with its own voice — that became the structural basis of the whole meditation.

Once *Ladoo* seemed to be finished, in 1976, Robert Bringhurst published it at Kanchenjunga Press. And I went out to do a reading in Vancouver. Robert had stayed up all night the night before, collating and stitching this handsome chapbook. But I had already revised the version he'd typeset, even though he'd only had it a few weeks. At the reading I could see him at the back of the hall, with fifty copies. I began to read — and suddenly he snatched up a copy and went riffling through it. "What the hell is Lee reading? I don't recognize this part at all!"

So yes, the long poems go through a lot of revision. With *Ladoo* it happened quickly, which is unusual for me. But if you looked at the manuscripts, you'd find the same old sordid story: thousands of pages of drafts, with fifteen lines gradually mutating to twenty pages. And with the poet shambling along behind, trying to catch up.

I I

You mentioned Simone Weil as a touchstone or influence. How important has she been to you?

I tried to read her for years, but I couldn't connect. Then something got through to me — probably *Gravity and Grace.* When I read her now, one minute I think I see what religious genius means in a way I never did before; and then two pages later I'm thinking, this is wacko. All that numerology, or the bizarre notions of . . . and then suddenly, wham! we're back into stuff that stops me dead in my tracks. So I'm wary but agog.

I'm tugged toward people who belong to the contemplative tradition, and specifically the strain called the negative way.

Weil is part of that, albeit in twentieth-century terms. I guess
the work that speaks to me the most in the high tradition is
The Cloud of Unknowing. But also Plotinus, Pseudo-Dionysus,
Meister Eckhart, John Tauler, Teresa of Avila, John of the
Cross.

And then there are people in recent centuries who were
intrinsically part of that tradition, though they didn't necessarily know all their forerunners. Hölderlin. Celan. Weil, as I
said. Eliot in *Four Quartets*. Heidegger — Heidegger is so
problematic. Believe me, this is not a list of the people I find
most cuddly. Half the moderns are crazies or bastards . . .
Merton, who was neither of those (though for a devotee of
silence, he sure went on). I'd also go to Beckett, Giacometti,
Rothko, Webern. Hector de Saint-Denys-Garneau is one of
the few Canadians I can identify. Nobody has made much
sense of this lineage in its modern phase, as far as I know. Most
of it falls outside the boundaries of conventional religion. And
I don't have it all straight, I just catch the affinities.

Anyway, that's the tradition I'm part of. The negative contemplative way. Majoring in poetry.

There's a line in Riffs, *"If I deny the luminous presence — /
something goes numb at the core." And that echoes throughout
your work. The gods have vanished, or we have banished them.
We live in a kind of limbo, with symbols and myths and hand-
me-downs and make-dos. But that power of divinity or spirituality, whatever word you put on it, is gone; yet it's something we
desperately need.*

You're right, that hunger is central to my stuff. Trying to talk
about it takes me outside poetry, though.

For twenty-five years, intuition has drawn me to cadence,
with the impulse to mime it in words — to polyphony as a
way of poetic knowing. But intuition also draws me to hunker
down in the "oblivion of eternity," as Leo Strauss or somebody calls the condition of deprival you speak of. Both those
vocations are second nature to me. But even though they're
intimately connected, they're not identical. "Knowing" stands

on its head when it comes to hunkering down in deprival; it stops meaning anything I recognize. But if you settle in deeply enough, that deprival can become a version of the negative path, the way of unknowing.

I'd like to get at what that feels like; what it is, to be summoned to a knowing outside of language altogether. A knowing outside of knowing. But for now I doubt I can do much more than clear the ground, point to the space where it arises. What the experience itself consists of, I'll barely broach — partly because I'm a beginner, partly because unknowing is intrinsically so hard to talk about. Maybe there's no reason to try.

When Eckhart or John of the Cross described the negative way, though, weren't they talking about something concrete? A specific kind of contemplative experience?

Absolutely. "The dark night of the soul" wasn't just a metaphor for going through a bad patch, though it's often used that way today.

First of all, it was about the experience of detachment, of being weaned from the need to possess things. And it happened in stages, or at least you can stylize it that way. John of the Cross spoke of the dark night of sense, where you gave up attachment to things of the world — money, belongings, bodily pleasure. And then the dark night of the soul, where you found religious consolations being stripped away too. Because the initial sweetness of contemplation had really been feeding a kind of spiritual materialism. Getting detached from possessiveness at that second level was a far more radical affair. Prayer went dry, God absconded, the works.

I remember stumbling into this tradition when I came across Eckhart in my teens, and feeling uncannily at home. The paraphernalia of late medieval Christianity, and then of the Counter-Reformation, which are two of the periods when it flourished, was about as alien as could be. (I was raised in the suburban United Church, so you can imagine.) But that experience of spiritual barrenness as sacramental, the claim of naughting, unknowing, the dazzling dark — there was an immediate *yes*. I was an outsider, but I came to it like entering my own skin . . . Mind you, my teens were much too early. After a few years I realized I was abusing it, turning something bedrock and sacred into my own little escapist fantasy, and I backed away. Even though what I was drawn to shaped my poetry from the beginning. And then I returned to it as a discipline in my mid-forties, at least for a while.

The traditional accounts are austere and breathtaking. It's wrong to paste ten-line summaries onto them, and I won't even try. But there's one element that brings you up short from the beginning. The classical negative way proceeded, not by a scintillating growth of spiritual insight and ecstasy, but by detachment *from* those things. It didn't matter if they happened to you, or if they never did. But it mattered that you would almost certainly take them for the goal, the object of the exercise. And that is what you had to relinquish — that spiritual attachment — till you were simply waiting on God in the darkness. Or waiting in darkness, period. Which is the primary modern experience of it.

Why did anyone choose to follow such a course? No one *chose* to. And neither — given that the whole landscape has changed past recognition — neither does anyone choose to now. It claims the people for whom it is right. Anyone else has a comparable challenge, to follow the path that's right for them.

For you, it sounds as if Catholic spirituality provided the framework for entering this way.

It wasn't that simple. The sense of recognition when I discovered the negative path — that was clearly a religious impulse. But traditional religious belief was not a possibility for me. There were believers galore in the world, and I respected a lot of them. But I couldn't join them. I realized that in my twenties, well before I had any notion of why. How did a person hold those things together, though — being naturally contemplative, and being a nonbeliever? And where did writing poetry fit in?

I got a bit of a leg up when I started to appreciate why classic statements of belief had so little purchase on me. Heidegger and Grant set me to pondering the mind-set I'd absorbed from university on; intellectually, it seemed, I had a textbook case of modernity. Even if I loathed it.

These matters are more widely understood now, but they were a revelation to me at the time. Let me sketch them in broad strokes.

After about 1600, a new cosmology developed in the West. Together with a new model of rational coherence, of how the mind finds order in the world. I'm not talking about Copernican astronomy or Newtonian physics, but rather the framework in which people made sense of them. Namely, the paradigm of "objective facts" and "subjective values" — with science exploring the patterns of order that configure the facts, and with the status of the values getting shakier and shakier over time.

And in the process the older, sacramental cosmos, where meaning or value inhered directly in what is, was retired to the museum. It could no longer be thought coherently by the educated mind. Within the categories that worked so well for analyzing the "objective" world we had invented, there was no provision for inherent meaning to exist at all. So conceptually, everything that exists was leeched of its tang and gist and quality — of the basic terms in which people once experienced it. (And still do, when we're not engaged in thinking about it.) Which undercut the central verities of Jerusalem and Athens and Rome: God, the Good, a chosen people, providence, heaven, the soul, the Trinity, the conscience, salvation. Even the "values" themselves, which were supposed to preserve some version of those things by herding them into a safe house of subjectivity, ended up being treated as value-free objects of study. We had no other model of what reason can *do*.

This doesn't mean that everyone who took science seriously rushed out to embrace a reductive, mechanistic worldview. That's one possible conjecture about what is. But that it can be demonstrated scientifically — that was the dream of a simpler time (though one that still finds adherents). In fact, scientists are just as apt to approach the world as a place of mystery, awe, even with a sort of mental gambler's delight. And to live by a code of right and wrong, and of the sanctity of truth, which they take as more than an arbitrary personal whim.

But if they do so, they're in the same boat as the rest of us who are denizens of modernity. We inhabit a cosmology whose rational categories do not let us parse the world — within those categories — as intrinsically awesome, or mysterious, or good and evil. Even if we experience the world in those terms; even if the experience is central to our lives. On the other hand, if we go back to the traditional languages of awe, their underlying assumptions affirm things which lie outside modern rational discourse. So our minds perforce go mute as a clam, if they try to address important matters in categories other *than* the modern . . . But is this really what our minds are good for? To fall mute in the face of what makes us centrally tick?

I don't speak of these things with any sense of being outside the quandary. The categories of my mind are drawn from our civilization's paradigm of rationality — how could they not be? So I wave at traditional belief across a wide divide. In fact, I wave at old-style belief *and* disbelief; classical atheism is nearly as inaccessible as classical theism. The unbelief of modernity is a new thing, a kind of atheism-by-default.

When I'm faced with premodern truths, then, it's as if someone has spoken to me in Urdu. They go on to ask, do I agree or disagree with what they just said? And I have to reply, "Sorry, I don't do either. I can't speak that language to begin with."

This account of the "oblivion of eternity" spoke to me deeply. And at the same time, though on a longer rhythm, I was recognizing something else. That is: it is fitting to be a citizen of secular modernity, and simultaneously to feel a great hunger. It's right to live in a world we understand as non-sacramental, and at the same time to recognize that you're not at home in it . . . Yes, you inhabit modernity. But as an alien. A Martian. A seeker.

Mind you, accepting that hunger still doesn't mean you can take refuge in the olden verities. Nor in New Age mumbo jumbo. Maybe not even in a wonderful foreign tradition like Zen; not, at least, if you mistrust your own capacity for self-indulgent tourism as much as I do. For better or worse, I'm a Westerner.

But those things said: it is apropos to be a secular modern, and to feel a hunger that the secular-modern world doesn't satisfy. You don't even need a label for the hunger, some rational category to legitimize it. Such categories are part of what *triggers* it in the first place. Just declaring yourself hungry in modernity, with no name for what you desire and no agenda beyond declaring it, is an act of dignity.

I should add that — surprise! — I do know such hunger, and take it as a life discipline. And at the same time I recognize that there are exemplary people, a majority I'm sure, who find reports of a nameless hunger thoroughly alien. Their way is different; for them to work up a hankering they don't feel would be daft. So if I explore a certain experience of incompleteness, of deep-down craving, I'm not suggesting it's the only matrix for living your life. It's just the one I know. . . .

Now we change gears. When you're young, you can afford to go haring after ideas like mad — even gloomy ideas. Why not? You're going to live forever. But when you hit middle age, there's a deeper crunch. If there's anything you've wanted with a passion, something vital you sense receding without your having tasted it, then merely stroking ideas *about* that thing feels dilettantish. You have to go for it firsthand. Or forget it. The clock is ticking in your body.

About seven years ago, I reached that point with the hunger I'm speaking of. Forget whatever I'd read in Heidegger and Grant; screw the Buddha and Jesus. I was *hungry*, and I wanted real food. Specifically, I wanted two things. To simplify my life. And to find a devotional practice — or else to discover, by looking, that I couldn't find one. I didn't know what either of those things would mean, but they were my leadings.

I won't dwell here on the urge to simplify. But what was the hunger for spiritual practice? . . . Well, when I can locate it, which is by no means all the time, the hunger is like a subsonic tug. It draws me to hush, to awe. I can feel it stirring at one remove when I'm out in the Shield, or listening to music, or making love. I imagine many people know it in comparable ways. In these cases, there's often a wonderful sense of hunger satisfied — though you recognize it *as* hunger only half a beat later, as the joy takes hold of your being. "I *needed* this! Even though I'd forgotten."

But often the tug is more direct — the impulse to awe pulls me immediately to stillness; draws me, with no intermediary, to centre and adore.

Adore what? I have no idea. The yen just breathes, the question is not germane. And simply to dwell in that hunger, not to tamp it down any longer — that's already a relief. In fact, in a way that's opaque to me, to dwell wholeheartedly in the hunger *is* somehow to "centre and adore." Indeed, to be partially fed. Not in any fashion I might have imagined; there's no sense of nourishment entering your system from outside. And if the whole thing transpires with no words or insights attached — well, welcome to spiritual life in the secular world. It means I'm called to worship without belief. For no reason, except I have to. In darkness; in muteness; in desire.

And without setting aside my nonbelief. What is just as primal as this awe is my inability to conceive a rationally credible *Something* that inspires it. I'm still a modern; my mind's not shaped that way. And there's also the moral outrage: how can evil get off scot-free? How can innocent people suffer so horribly? . . . But what I came to see was that those things don't invalidate the hunger. Rather, they set the conditions for what you can do about it. I may be unable to pray to God. But I can sit still, in awe and desire; and I can stop trying to possess what leads me to do so. Even by wanting to know it.

Here's something that speaks for this unnameable hunger; something that gave me the shock of recognition when I came across it. It was written around 1370, in England, in *The Cloud of Unknowing*: "It is not your will or desire that moves you, but something you are completely ignorant of, stirring you to will and desire you know not what. Please do not worry if you never know more than this . . ."

For people on other paths, that may be just a bunch of words. But if you realize you know what the words are pointing to; if you already recognize that sense of obscure, almost pre-personal arousal, of being stirred and claimed at a level so intimate you hadn't consciously known it was there — and without being able to identify what's doing the claiming, or even to bring it into focus as something separate from yourself — then the words go right to the quick. You *know* this experience of hunger, even though you never knew you did.

You can live in that hunger as home. It's roomy enough. It's sheer eros, to use the old language. What's harder to convey, without merely trafficking in ideas, is what comes with it. The realization that "I" will never stop feeling hungry, or trying to possess. That "I" is specious to begin with, though it won't go away. That there is a deeper hunger feast — and a durable yes and agony — to which access is real.

There are themes here that interest many contemporary thinkers: the limits of reason, the struggle to express things which are inexpressible, the question whether we can know anything outside the shaping categories of language. How much have you drawn from other writers who explore these ideas?

Well, when you put it that way: as little as possible. Remember that I'm pursuing this as a starving man, not a "contemporary thinker." I can't say whether anyone else is following their right path. But for me, it would be dead wrong to take all this as so many themes and ideas. That would simply reproduce the impasse.

And by now, surely, thinking about the impotence of thought toward meaning is worthwhile only if you *stop* "thinking" about it. The experience itself has to become a discipline of mortification — lead you out of ideas into actively dwelling in hunger. Not just into more ideas *about* dwelling in hunger. And in fact that direct, unmediated dwelling is the only kind of practice open to someone like me.

Let me expand on this. There have been several devotional traditions in the West. By "devotional," I mean a daily practice of quiet time that starts to shape your life — maybe fifteen minutes a day, maybe two hours. Maybe all day, at a subterranean level. And in the dominant Western tradition, the "affirmative way," you focus in these times on inspirational scenes from the Bible, revealed theological truths, or some other positive religious content. But that form of devotion was off limits for me from the start. All a person with a modern mind-set is going to do, in devotions of that kind, is argue with the assumptions of the exemplary material. It's hypocritical to nod along piously with the old truths, if you live in a world in which they're un-thinkable. But if you're just going to listen to yourself carry on a debate, the whole exercise is a waste of time. You could be out stealing hubcaps, doing something useful.

So there's no entry, for me, to the affirmative way. In traditional terms, this amounts to saying that a modern is denied access to meditation. He has to begin — if he's called to devotional practice at all — at the stage of contemplation.

This too I should expand on. In the devotional life, "meditation" refers to the earlier stages of spiritual practice, where a person focuses by conscious will on the kind of positive content I spoke of. (This use of the term is not the same as in "meditative poetry," though the two aren't entirely dissimilar.) But in some cases, at least, a person who practises meditation finds himself being led deeper. The content drops away, in the course of weeks or months or years, and he is claimed by a wordless and thought-free attending. Here, your will is important only as a means of letting go of willing, so that (in traditional terms) God can take the initiative. It's this later stage which is properly called contemplation.

It's disconcerting to realize that this is the entry point you have to begin at, if all you can do in positive meditation is carry on a debate. It's like finding that you're obliged to walk before you've learned how to crawl. All kinds of things can go wrong, especially if you don't have a spiritual director or friend. Mind you, you make this discovery only if you have to; reading about various stages and ways won't get you there. So if you're not meant for contemplation, you drop out soon enough.

What then? Well, there's a funny turnaround here, which is hard to articulate. Our version of rationality has rendered the world *so* heroically knowable, and *so* alien; and meanwhile we are hungry at the core. In the result, a brain-cracking detachment from brain knowledge has been accomplished — impersonally, at the civilizational level. For the enlightened, this may always have been the case. But before modernity, such a gridlock of the mind was something a person stumbled upon individually. It wasn't a fact of the public landscape, as out-there as strip mines and shopping plazas.

Let me take another crack at this; it's a whole gestalt I'm reaching for, it's hard to get it all said at once . . . There are crucial possibilities for thinking which are not available within modernity. I spoke of the impossibility of rationally parsing the world as awesome. But as another instance: if we reflect on Nazism, we *know* we have to say — in whatever terms we use — "This was evil." If we can't make that judgement, we are not adequately human. But that is precisely the kind of statement which the best modern knowing has ruled out. We're allowed to say, "I feel a subjective loathing for Adolf Hitler." Or we can declare, "Nazism contradicted the value-systems that have been normative in Western societies." But the bedrock moral revulsion of "This is evil" — we may know that imperative still, but as moderns we can't articulate it.

Why not? Because "evil" is no longer a rational category we have access to. Not as anything but a relative term, whose content is defined historically. We know how to compare the meanings assigned to "evil" in societies with different value systems. That's what the modern paradigm equips us to do. But that is not how our substance cries out to respond to Nazism — by cranking out yet another "value-free" study in relative values. Fortunately, we can still act on our sense of good and evil. But within the categories of modern reason, we can't *think* "good and evil." Not as craggy, magisterial reality, with a claim on us as primal as that of objective knowing or subjective feeling. Maybe more primal still.

So a profound sense of things is gagged. And this muting at the core is hardly a trivial lack. What we hunger for as humans, and what our rational minds can know, are disjunct — to the point that it becomes a schizophrenia of the species. And over the past centuries, it's the hunger for meaning, for good, that has gone into the closet. There has been no intellectually respectable way to coax it back out.

And that's why, when I realized I felt at home in the negative way, the fit seemed uncanny. I mean the fit between this larger condition of rationally stymied deprival, which we now inherit by birthright, and a devotional practice where hunger is taken for granted, and daily contemplation is taken for granted — but where you're specifically enjoined *not* to try to "reach God" through spiritual exercises. Where content-laden religious reflections have to be renounced just as fully as everything else; letting them go is itself a devotional exercise. And where you wait stripped, in "naked intent," claimed by you-can't-say-what. Or not claimed, since you don't have control. In eros, unknowing, and awe.

This felt like home. It felt like a way that opens naturally within the reflexes available to a Westerner and denizen of unbelief. I'm not going to trundle out my own kindergarten experience of the negative way here, nor my attempts to find a community that shares this practice. But in the older tradition there was a body of lived knowledge, a practical lore, whose experimental bite I discovered for myself.

Mind you, I can't ignore a fundamental shift. Before the modern era, people who were claimed by unknowing still lived in a sacramental cosmology. At some level inaccessible to us, they moved in a climate of belief. You can't just rejig them now into proto-secular moderns, enlist them as good old skeptical buddies. They weren't, even if they found themselves drawn beyond "belief." But still there is an opening into the way they took, for someone today who is blindsided by awe, and barred from belief, and prepared to change his life. That much I know. And odd though it sounds, why shouldn't a contemplative path open in a secular age as much as in a religious one? If it's for real, it doesn't depend on the mental paradigms of a particular era. You don't have to be a believer to be hauled down by awe.

In fact — I'm speaking more speculatively now — perhaps this is the next step in the whole project of reason. A fate. What thought has arrived at. That after centuries of its brilliant, catastrophic ascendancy, a thinker now sit in silence, daily, quick as a hunger pang. Attending in wordless desire. Perhaps that discipline carries the logic of modern reason to its own next stage.

Of course, this doesn't falsify particular scientific observations or theories. That would be fatuous, it's not what unknowing is about. It is rather a matter of letting the reflexes of our beautiful rationality discover the checkmate that belongs to them, simultaneous with their near-omnipotence. Letting them be matter-of-factly boggled. And waiting on what comes next.

Our form of reason *is* impotent toward meaning. But mind doesn't need yet another speculative elaboration of its triumphant dead-end. It needs the chance to sit, and love through its own eclipse. And eventually, I believe, it needs to find another form of reason.

I I I

How does that discipline connect with writing poetry?

Oh man, that's a doozer. Polyphony and dark knowing: beautiful doozers. I still haven't got it straight.

I know that writing poetry, and secular contemplation in the negative way — for me they're intimates. Both proceed intuitively. Both start by moving into a space of darkness, silence, attending. Both are life disciplines. And they don't own anything; at best, they're claimed by small openings.

But they're so different, too. What is the relation between kinaesthetic cadence — which I know in a meat-and-potatoes way, even if it's obscure knowing — what is the relation between cadence and the ground of unknowing, where in practice I'm so radically disoriented I can't even be sure that "ground of unknowing" refers *to* "something" at all? Are they the same thing? Two separate realities? I don't know how they relate.

And I don't even know the right mesh between the two activities. Sometimes I can practise both, sometimes one or the other falls away. These days I write.

I'd better just acknowledge the question, and let it breathe.

Body Music

Notes on Rhythm in Poetry

1.

What makes a poem cohere? How does it mean what it means?

It starts where the poem does: in the pre-verbal flex and coherence the words arise from. A poem tries to enact that wordless tumble and surge in its own medium — in line breaks and pauses, syntax and sound, the ripple and clarion strut of sense on the page. Through the nitty-gritty of craft, it tries to recreate the cadence of how things are.

But how do you get a handle on that? How can you understand technique as more than just a bag of tricks? As witness, and cosmology, and desire?

2.

It starts with rhythm, that much I know. I mean the way the poem moves in time — its pace and gait and proportions. A poem can unfold with the shapely aplomb of a gavotte, or meander, or move with a quicksilver stutter and glide. Each rhythm shapes the energy flow with a distinct logic; each parses the world with a syntax of its own. A poem thinks by the way it moves.

But that raises another question, for this logic is not conceptual. How can you translate its native terms into categories your mind can deal with? How do you talk about rhythmic moves your body grasps in a flash?

3.

I'm drawn to terms like these.

Prosody as sonic improvisation. Polyrhythmic form. A kinetics of meaning: clenched, a galumph, then wash of a liminal segue. Forward momentum; lateral gusts. Kinaesthetic knowing. Trajectories in audio space. Scoring the energy spoor. The rhythmic manifold. A poetics of voice in motion. Cosmophony. Body music.

4.

Acts of rhythmic attention comprise a syntax for knowing the world.

5.

How do we apprehend rhythm?

It's customary to take the auditory sense as primary. We "hear the beat," we say — and so we do. But that's too restricted. We need to include the rhythmic experience of the whole body. This involves hearing, and sometimes sight and touch. But more fundamentally, it involves the way our muscles register pressure, torsion, stress, pulsation, movement; the way they distinguish a throb from a lurch from a zoom.

We experience texture and periodicity right at the muscular level — with our kinaesthetic sense. Our body becomes the instrument the rhythm is played on; we register it viscerally, absorb it as carnal knowledge.

★

And we know a certain inner experience, which unfolds with no external stimulus to the organ involved. Thus we "hear with our inner ear," we "see with the third eye." Most of us could listen to a favourite song right now inside our heads, and talk about the experience. This faculty is vital when it comes to poetry — and nowhere more than with the muscular sense. We can experience a tumble and carom and surge without physical prompting, as I can attest. Yet the faculty has no name, informal or technical.

What to call this intuitive kinaesthetic sense — *kine-sense? body music? kintuition?* I don't know the right term yet, but the faculty is normative.

6.

How we scan the world.

How a poem's music makes a statement of its own — before, beneath, and shot-through the particular content. A second language.

It says: the world comes in chunks. Or *glissando*. Or, there is a deep current. Or a hush. Or cacophony. It says . . .

7.

Prosody rhymes with cosmology. I know that's so, but I can't yet say what it means.

8.

I remember poring over Pound and Williams in the early sixties. The way their poems moved — what the hell were they *doing*? I found their rhythms foreign, since my ear had been shaped by traditional poetry. Yet I knew I had to connect. I was trying to write, but my hunches didn't jibe with the older rhythmic language.

By the time I caught up with my immediate elders, Purdy and Creeley & Co., I'd begun to acclimatize to the modern soundscape. Mind you, most poets of my generation had been attuned to it for years. But I didn't feel an automatic rapport with their body music. And when I did, it was scary. I opened John Newlove's *Moving in Alone* in 1965, and I wanted to kneecap the man. Assassinate him. Here was a poet my own age, with moves so cleanly etched I could feel them probing the reflexes of my work, exposing its mannered stiffness. How had he learned to write like that?

Since then I've found my way to a kinaesthetic language that feels more like home. But when I test the poetic rhythms of the last hundred years — body-scan them, so to speak — I still get mixed signals. There are modes that feel continuous with the way things are. There are others that feel alien. And there are rhythms I know firsthand that don't show up in the accepted accounts at all.

That's part of what I want to reckon with now: this inside/outside relation to the norms of modern rhythm.

9.

There is a craft of scoring energy on the page. You orchestrate the flow; you coax it to enact the dance.

10.

The poetry I mean to explore exists first of all on the page; its native medium is print.

One thing is so obvious, it's seldom discussed. That is, while page poetry is a temporal medium, its sequence unfolds in space as well as time. A poem's specific rhythms emerge when you start at line one, read from left to right, and make your way down the page to the end. The poem unfolds in time, but its unfolding is enacted in space; the two dimensions are interdependent.

But the ratio of interdependence is not a constant. In classical English poetry, the spatial dimension seldom claims our attention. In modern poetry, by contrast, temporal and spatial aspects are conspicuously fused. The rhythms of a modern poem could not exist outside its spatial dimension.

But I'm jumping ahead. For now, it's enough to observe that poetic rhythm unfolds in spatio-temporal terms.

11.

The order you sense in cadence is more like a passage of music, or a movement of dance, than a geometrical figure.

200

What the poem mimes is not a static structure, but an active cohering. Kinetic rhythms of being. A cosmophony, more than a cosmology.

12.

You can chart the history of poetry on a rhythmic axis.

In the mid-nineteenth century, a few poets began to chafe at the grammar of rhythmic coherence which had obtained for hundreds of years. Working in isolation, the best found alternative rhythms. And in the first two decades of the twentieth, the process reached a crescendo, creating a new rhythmic logic for poetry. This paralleled developments in other fields — physics, music, painting — where the basic grammar of coherence was likewise being transformed. "Modern poetry" means poetry which participates in this transformation of rhythmic norms.

The transformation was achieved in the composition of particular poems. Critical analysis is still catching up.

*

* *Classical English poetry.* Poetry written in traditional rhythmic syntax. Classical poetry extends, with many permutations, from Chaucer to the present.

* *Modern English poetry.* Poetry that works with a range of non-classical rhythmic intuitions. It extends from at least Whitman to the present; thus it overlaps in time with recent classical poetry. And many poets now use rhythmic conventions from both traditions. (The usage is different from "modern thought," which refers to the form and content of thinking since about 1600.)

* *Modernist poetry.* The first fully developed generation of modern poetry — Pound, Eliot, Williams, etc. The high period was roughly 1915–50. Because of a particular technical advance which we'll come to soon, we can say that the modernists initiated modern poetry proper.

13.

You steer by your ear. By your kinaesthetic ear.

There are actual rhythms, in known poems, that are world-instigating. But some don't appear on the orthodox maps of the rhythmic continuum. What's more, there are modern rhythms that have yet to be enacted.

We have only begun to explore this new acoustic space.

14.

Rich rhythmic manifold: how to score the plenum? The frequencies of being?

The dance of simultaneous wavelengths — how to honour them at once?

15.

In a poem of any length, different kinds of rhythm unfold simultaneously. They operate at different scales, each with its own language. As a working distinction:

- *Micro-rhythms*: the fine-scale rhythms that organize syllables, words, a line, several lines.

- *Mezzo-rhythms*: the rhythms that obtain on a middle scale — from several lines to half a page. (As an example, the rhythms of a stanza or a verse paragraph.)

- *Macro-rhythms*: the rhythms that orchestrate parts within the whole.

16.

It starts with *prosody*. The fundamental rhythmic syntax.

There are dictionary definitions, all of them based on classical practice. But for our present purposes, they're too narrow. What I mean by prosody is *the craft of orchestrating micro-rhythms*.

★

Why start with prosody?

Because it's the basis for everything else. The deep matrix. You can't write a two-page poem without a feel for macro-rhythms. But without a feel for micro-rhythms, you can't write two lines. The poem's shoelaces are tied together; six words on a page just sit there — or they clunk along, an arbitrary sequence of syllables.

★

In classical English poetry, micro-rhythms were organized by metrical prosody. In modern poetry, they're organized on a different basis.

Arriving at a new prosody was the basic technical step in the invention of modern poetry, the most profoundly enabling. And it was part of a general shift in our intuition of coherence.

That larger shift intrigues me, though I'll concentrate here on its manifestation in poetry.

17.

To fathom metrical prosody, you can't just rehearse the scansion of specific feet and meters, like we did in grade ten. Nor simply retrace the history of its development since 1400, compelling though that is. You have to explore how poets were *using* this rhythmic language: how it let them scan the world. And what they heard.

18.

The basis of metrical prosody was a particular element of rhythm: the stress or intensity with which we pronounce individual syllables. Traditionally, two degrees of intensity were recognized — strong and weak. The micro-rhythm of classical English poetry was based on the organization of strong and weak syllabic stresses.

But you have to go further than that. As I understand it, metrical prosody was a craft of improvisation, in which two different systems of syllabic stress were syncopated against each other. Two "protocols," I'll call them (since one was not a system at all). One protocol was fixed, the other variable.

The fixed protocol was the meter, or "measure." It gave an abstract model for the rhythm of each line — a pre-established sequence of strong and weak beats. Iambic pentameter, trochaic tetrameter, whatever. Each meter consisted of x-many feet, or syllabic units. And since it repeated the same foot throughout, the metrical rhythm was regular.

A reader recognized this underlying measure in the first few lines — kinaesthetically, not analytically. Its beat went on ticking in the reader's body sense for the rest of the poem, like a ghostly metronome. (In iambic pentameter: *da-DUM / da-DUM / da-DUM / da-DUM / da-DUM*.) And this furnished the ground bass for whatever syllabic rhythms actually ensued. The distinction is important, since no poet reproduced the metrical pattern beat for beat unless he was very naive.

The second, variable protocol consisted of the stresses found in the actual words of the poem — pronounced as they are in ordinary speech. This protocol was unprogrammed, and irregular. Some of its stresses coincided with the metrical beat (weak or strong); others diverged from it. But providing they didn't deviate for too long, the reader continued to sense the meter ticking.

What metrical poets developed was a craft of *syncopation*: of counterpointing the flux of spoken stresses against the regular metrical beat, so they kept dancing in and out of phase in the reader's body sense. This syncopation unfolded largely beneath his threshold of conscious attention, keeping the subliminal micro-rhythms carnal and vivacious. The more resourceful the poet, the more compelling the dance.

19.

The sophistication and richness of metrical craft take my breath away. Even though it's not my native language, except in children's poetry.

20.

The natural unit of meter was the line. So you can observe
the prosody at work by auditing a single line:

Let me not to the marriage of true minds . . .

You pick up the syncopation most readily if you try inflect-
ing the line by the iambic pattern alone, and observe the
nonsensical singsong that results:

Let ME / not TO / the MAR- / (ri)age OF / true MINDS . . .

That's grotesque. But nobody reads the line that way. And
when you speak it more naturally — however you inflect it
exactly; there's no single right way, which means the reader
too must improvise — the spoken stresses and the metrical
beat move in and out of phase. The strong accent may shift
to a different position within a foot. Three syllables will skip
along in the metrical space reserved for two. There may be no
strong spoken stress at all in a syllabic group where the meter
makes us hear one. There are speed-ups and hesitations. The
syncopated micro-rhythms emerge as shifting and alive.

★

What determines the moment-to-moment syncopation?
At one level, it's simply the standard pronunciation of words
— which coincides with the metrical beat for a foot or two,
then sets up a counter-rhythm, then returns to the meter. But
since nothing obliged the poet to use precisely these words,
the explanation is correct but beside the point.
Finally, all you can say is that some deep, spontaneous
delight in improvisation configures the micro-rhythms. Kintuition, I'll call it. Kinaesthetic play.

21.

What sense of coherence is manifest here?
It's possible to discern signature moves in the prosody of
individual poets, and these enact the syntax of order that each

intuits. But going further: how is coherence parsed in metrical prosody at large? What underlying scansion of the world does it embody?

It says, there is a fixed order. And at the same time, there is a flux: of freedom, of chaos, of both. Truth in rhythm consists of orchestrating order and flux at once.

Two rhythmic protocols: one fixed, one variable. Without meter, measure, degree — without some residual sense of natural law, holding the world together — the freeplay of particulars would degenerate into chaos. Without unscheduled play, structure would become an iron grid. It is within this kintuition, of established order and freedom entwined, that rhythmic meaning emerges in metrical poetry.

For centuries, this cosmophony governed the micro-rhythm of poetry. And in broad terms, it seems to me, it meshed with the sense of the world's coherence which persisted in Europe during its ascendancy: the sense that things were free to be themselves within the natural law established by God.

22.

That was one kintuition of coherence. But the centre ceased to hold; in the body sense of more and more poets, the world no longer moved that way. And that intrigues me. What were they picking up? How did they know what they knew?

Whatever the explanation, a crisis in rhythmic norms ensued. After 1850, some poets began to grope for a different syntax of micro-rhythms. This produced a flurry of unrelated experiments in prosody, some of them non-metrical. But sixty years later, even the best remained isolated achievements. They were like beautiful, sideways evolutionary mutations — each of which had established a niche of its own, but none of which became the primary line of development.

*

The most important innovations were Whitman's dithyrambic line, and Hopkins' sprung verse. But Hopkins was unrepeatable. And while Whitman's line tantalized later poets, it swamped almost everyone who tried it; only Lawrence, Jeffers, Ginsberg would find their own way.

Other new prosodies were arbitrary, like the non-metrical syllabics which Marianne Moore would devise. And there was a scatter of backward-looking experiments. Some poets tried to modify the status quo by exhuming Latin meter. And around 1910, Eliot developed his own subtle modification of metrical prosody.

All these mutations bubbled up in the shift from classical to modern micro-rhythm. In the case of Whitman, Hopkins, Eliot, the new prosodies engendered great poetry, but mainly by their creators. None of them furnished a rhythmic language which poets of widely varied persuasions could use. And the other innovations were sports, or tours de force, rather than live new rhythmic languages.

★

If we freeze the frame in 1910, we get this picture. It was still possible for poets of the first rank to work in meter — as Yeats was doing, and Stevens later would. But for the growing number of poets who had lost access to that language, there was no prosody that let them move naturally on the page.

23.

Losing pentameter wasn't the problem. The problem was, losing iambic. With the metronome gone, the syllable came unmoored.

24.

It's not surprising that some poets tried to cope by tinkering with traditional prosody. To give up meter altogether, without some potent alternative galvanizing you — that brought on vertigo. There was nothing to steer by. Consider:

Without that steady underbeat as the norm, what governs the rhythm of syllables? Is there any music left that's specific to poetry? Aren't you just writing prose, chopped into shorter and longer lines?

What *is* a line of verse, when there's no fixed measure? How do you know where to end one string of words and start the next? If you can break a line after the tenth word, why not after the eighth? or the second? Why not divide it into ten itty-bitty lines, each of a single word?

The more deeply you enter post-metrical listening, the blurrier things get. The left-hand margin, for instance: what anchors it now? If you're no longer heading back to that fixed point to start a new metrical run, what necessity does it have? Why should a line start at the far left? Why should it start in *any* specific position? But if it's cut adrift, where does it come to rest? The whole prosodic logic of the poem has become impossibly fluid. The white space of the page starts to feel like a deeper-breathing silence, with this aimless welter of words slipsliding around in it.

Without meter, what is the basis of rhythmic coherence — *any* basis? *any* coherence? How should syllables move on the page? Put differently: how does the world cohere? What are the categories in which it makes sense? Or are there any?

25.

The breakthrough came with the discovery of free verse.

The term has a varied history. But I take it to mean poetry written in a new prosody, which Ezra Pound developed beween 1912 and 1920 (following French examples, and experiments by Hilda Doolittle). The system spread like gossip, becoming the non-metrical prosody of choice in the English-speaking world. It embodied a new kintuition of order.

26.

I call this new system *scoring*, or *free prosody*. Poets have been using it for almost a century now. But deciphering how it works is still a challenge.

If I've got it straight, scoring proceeds by syncopating two rhythmic protocols, as metrical prosody did. But there the resemblance ends. You can't understand scoring by looking for equivalents to metrical categories; it's an entirely different way of hearing micro-rhythm.

      ★

In broad terms, its features are these:

One rhythmic protocol draws on patterns of speech; the other depends on line breaks and layout on the page. These can be termed syntax and notation respectively.

Both protocols are variable. That is, the prosody is free.

The focus is not on syllabic stress, but on "pointing." On the rhythms of local attention. When the two protocols are syncopated, the pointing of one is played against the pointing of the other.

The natural unit of scoring is not the line, but a sequence of two or more lines.

In this vocabulary: scoring improvises the pointing of micro-rhythms, through the interplay of syntax and notation.

27.

A director "points" the flow of a scene on the stage. A violinist points a passage of a sonata. They etch the rhythms cleanly, bring out specific textures and dynamics. Otherwise the performance is muddy, lumpy, lacks focus.

Pointing controls for two things: pacing and emphasis. Pacing includes speed — slower or faster; momentum — the force of advance; tempo — the cumulative changes in speed and momentum. And emphasis includes the darts or swirls of attention which guide us to focus on *this* word, *this* moment, *this* pool of feeling, and to glide past others.

When a passage is pointed well, it's impossible to say where pacing ends and emphasis begins. They're different names for the same dynamics.

      ★

Mind you, a live performance has resources for pointing which don't exist on the page. Volume and timbre and pitch; physical movement; body language. A page poem would kill for them, but it can't have them. It has other things instead.

28.

What do the protocols of pointing in free prosody consist of?

We know what we mean by syntax: the arrangement of grammatical parts in a sentence. The way subject and verb and object organize what's being expressed; the way phrases and clauses are massed and counterweighted. The syntax points the meaning with a specific kinetic logic.

And I'll expand the term, to include the way consecutive sentences are marshalled. That creates a further range of syntactic pointing. Two quick sentences, leading to a mighty periodic surge. Staccato question: staccato reply. If the words are savvy, their syntax guides us through a specific rhythm of attention

*

But what determines the syntax of a free poem?

That's like asking what governs the spoken stresses in a metrical poem. In a sense, both are generated by the content. But that's just the point of departure. The poet is goosed along by an intuitive *something* — in scoring, to jump ahead, by the rhythmic dance that's itching to happen, if he can get the syntax talking to the notation the way they're straining to.

What generates the syntax is the open-ended tug and *telos* of improvisation. No recipes; no nets.

Finally, it is governed by the poet's kintuition of cadence. By the tumble and play of what is. The body music of world.

29.

What about the pointing created by notation?

As we saw above, in post-metrical poetry you can point the words in a dizzying variety of ways, depending on how you set them up on the page. The pacing and emphasis change as you vary the spatial layout, sometimes dramatically, sometimes almost imperceptibly. Yet the actual elements of notation are few in number.

The basic element is the line break. Its placement determines the length of the line. It also affects the pace: speeding it up, slowing it down, shifting it from measured to headlong. And it affects the emphasis, particularly if the break comes in the middle of a unit of sense; a slightly heightened stress falls on the first word of the next line. Many free-verse poets notate exclusively with line breaks.

If they go further, the next element is the margin: which lines to indent; how far. This sets up an additional level of pointing, creating parallel or off-centre relationships among the lines. And it affects the pace, because it governs the return time: how long it takes the eye to swing back to the beginning of the next line.

Two other elements appear less frequently: internal spaces within a line, and deployment of the white space of the page as an active component, connoting silence.

30.

To hear free prosody at work, you have to listen to several lines. Here's Pound in the *Pisan Cantos*, scoring open notation against the syntax:

> . . . and the news is a long time moving
> a long time in arriving
> thru the impenetrable
> crystalline, indestructable
> ignorance of locality
> The news was quicker in Troy's time
> a match on Cnidos, a glow worm on Mitylene . . .

The syntax points the sense with a deliberate, measured movement, as the three sets of parallel phrases unfold. And at the same time, the line breaks and staggered margins point the sense with a second logic — which sometimes meshes with the syntax, sometimes plays across it. The two protocols marry on the page, creating a flow of rhythmic attention which is almost liturgical, yet locally alive.

No other poem will repeat this particular scoring; each move in free prosody is a one-shot improvisation. But the language of syntax-and-notation is wonderfully flexible. It's hard to do well, but it allows a poet room to orchestrate micro-rhythms in the key of whatever. It gives poets of many different persuasions a language to work in.

31.

This account of scoring leaves several loose ends to sort out.

When you read a free poem out loud, it's often difficult to translate the spatial notation into physical sound. Line breaks are dicey; indents are impossible. As a result, much of the pointing gets flattened out in a live reading. It is fully accessible only in the original, spatio-temporal medium, where the notation can be seen.

At the same time, there are new resources when you read aloud, such as volume and pitch. A free poem is aural, but on the page it can only gesture at some of its own vocal shading.

This means that to experience a free poem in its home medium, you have to *hear it out loud on the page*. You have to absorb its movement with the eye, the inner ear, and the body sense at once.

32.

In the passage from Pound, the last line was in iambic pentameter: "a match on Cnidos, a glow worm on Mitylene." We sense the five-beat pattern behind the words; each reader will syncopate the spoken stresses against that abstract measure in his own way.

But if the poem is in free verse, how can this be?

There's no law against shifting into meter in free verse. Some poets never do; others do for a phrase, a line, even a short passage. But when this happens, how should we specify the prosody? I understand it thus:

The poem's entire movement is governed by free prosody. It is scored throughout.

When it passes through a metrical patch, it's both scored and metrical. Within that local domain, it obeys both prosodies at once.

In a comparable way, the laws of Newtonian space obtain locally within Einsteinian space-time.

33.

In free verse, syllables are stressed as they are in metrical poetry — by their spoken pronunciation. This brings something else to light.

There are only so many patterns that syllabic stresses can fall into; hence you still find dactyls and spondees and iambs in free verse. But these are not metrical feet. They are something we don't have a name for yet: units of spoken stress.

These patterns of emphasis can be artfully deployed in a poem, but that doesn't mean they're being syncopated against a background meter. The whole telephone book can be analyzed into spoken iambs and trochees and anapests; it's still not a metrical composition. It is only when a line is unmistakably syncopated against a known meter — "a match on Cnidos, a glow worm on Mitylene" — that it is metrical.

34.

This brings us to the primary question: how is coherence parsed in free prosody? Beyond the signature moves of individual poets, what scansion of the world does it enact?

What's new in free prosody is that there is no fixed measure. Both protocols are variable. And while each can become regular for a spell, that is simply one possibility within the rhythmic continuum. It doesn't define the continuum *per se*.

Free prosody says, the world is coherent — but its coherence emerges in the interplay of variable systems of order. There is no absolute measure which antedates the poem. Coherence is local, provisional, contingent in the flux.

This is a new kintuition of order: polyvalent and relative. It gives the distinctive cosmophony of modern rhythm. And in ways I can glimpse, if only dimly, it meshes with the account of the world's coherence which has emerged in the last century. It resonates with the formal intuitions of relativity and quantum mechanics, where an absolute frame of reference no longer exists.

35.

It's time to sharpen some distinctions:

Kinaesthesia: the sensation in the muscles produced by direct physical pressure, movement, pulsation.

Body music: the inner experience of kinaesthetic rhythm, when there is no literal stimulus to the muscles. The occasion may be reading a poem, or listening to music. Or it can be triggered by memory or kintuition.

Kintuition: kinaesthetic intuition. The capacity to register rhythm with no identifiable mediation, direct or indirect. This might sound like mystification, if it weren't the normal working experience of many artists.

*

I also use "body music" in two extended senses:

The kinaesthetic dimension of a poem.

The rhythmic coherence of what is. The body music of world. Cadence; cosmophony. It is to this, I believe, that kintuition responds.

36.

Rich rhythmic manifold: how to score the plenum?

Acts of rhythmic attention are a species of natural prayer.
Cosmophony and desire.

37.

The modernist innovators discovered a brave new rhythmic
world. But it was not exhaustively defined by the poems they
wrote, nor the theories they devised.

What's more, our current map of the modern tradition —
which shows it originating with Whitman, coming into its
own in Pound, Eliot, and Williams, and then fanning out
through the ramifications of the new American poetry — is
not a trustworthy guide. Or not, at least, when it comes to
modern rhythm at the mezzo- and macro-scales. That account
identifies achievements which are there, and deserve to be
celebrated. But it closes off the continuum of rhythmic possibilities to a claustrophobic degree.

38.

Radio space. The air alive with waves, vibrations.

So too there are frequencies of being.

Step 1: a way of moving that can tune to this plural energy,
and let it shape the movement of the poem. Enacting first one
frequency, then another, then the next.

Step 1002: what makes you crazy — how to write the world
as it *is*. Not consecutive, but overlaid. How cadence teems on
simultaneous wavelengths: slalom and moloch and crouch.
And torque. *And* soar . . .

The challenge is, how to enact a polyrhythmic body music?

39.

It's the all-at-onceness that gets you. When you're attuned,
the many-plied rhythms issue an impossible directive: utter
us utterly. Dance all of us — now, in words, at once.

It is in light of that kintuition that a poem of any length

works for me or doesn't. Before I attend to anything else, I crave a music that inhabits polyrhythm as a denizen.

But how to honour that directive on the page?

40.

I want now to jostle our map of sonic space, to make a particular mezzo-rhythm audible.

Anyone who has been claimed by the moves I speak of will know why they matter. They coexist with the rhythms of prosody. But they organize the trajectory of the poem on a larger scale, in passages of ten or twenty lines. And they employ an entirely different rhythmic language.

41.

The mezzo-rhythm I have in mind is what I call *compound rhythm*. Or *composite movement*. Or *forward/lateral action*.

In broad terms, it occurs when one energy propels the poem down the page — and gets simultaneously buffeted, transsected, deformed by a series of lateral gusts. These cross-energies multiply the flow, and redirect the original momentum. The effect is to make us experience two or more energies at once: to make the poem polyrhythmic. We start to hear what could be called "rhythmic harmonics."

★

Take a relatively straightforward example, still in general terms. Suppose one train of thought is underway. And suppose it is invaded — conceptually and syntactically — by a second train of thought, which comes in from a different angle. The poem assimilates this incursion, and continues its (altered) course. As it does, we feel the new thought powering the advance at the same time as the original. Both energies, forward and lateral, now propel the poem; its rhythm is compound.

And the energies don't have to be conceptual. There may be a tidal wave of feeling — of celebration, perhaps — which

216

surges ahead in cresting rhythms. Yet a series of nagging underfeelings begin to declare themselves, cutting across the ongoing flow with dissident moves and tonalities.

Or the poem proceeds by a series of minute discriminations — but then gets blindsided by a larger prophetic afflatus. Or a blurt of grief. Or whatever. Both modes of locomotion continue as the poem proceeds.

These lateral dynamics can be of any kind: shifts of voice; sudden memories; associative musings, touched off by something as slight as a double take on the sound of a word. They are heterogeneous in nature. And the crosshatched energies begin to mime the plenum, the polyphasic cadence of what is.

42.

Who has written this way? This amounts to asking, what would a truer map of rhythmic ancestors look like? When I scan the continuum with that in mind, it leads me outside English poetry.

As far as I can tell, the first modern master of compound mezzo-rhythm was Friedrich Hölderlin. Starting in the late 1790s, his freefall through a new cadential space was enacted so potently on the page, I can give pride of ancestral place to no one but him. The stricken tremendum he tracked in his elegies and odes is kinaesthetically richer than much of what has happened since. Our map of usable ancestors should be expanded to recognize his polyrhythmic innovations.

*

No short excerpt can do justice to Hölderlin's body music. But here is one stanza from "Patmos." He is speaking of the death of Christ, and the subsequent withdrawal of the sacred from the daily world. Beyond the content, however, the rhythm tells a story of its own. A torrential energy hurtles down the page; at the same time, cross-energies swarm — splaying the syntax, and dissolving normal connectives:

Wenn aber stirbt alsdenn
An dem am meisten
Die Schönheit hing, dass an der Gestalt
Ein Wunder war und die Himmlischen gedeutet
Auf ihn, und wenn, ein Rätsel ewig füreinander,
Sie sich nicht fassen können
Einander, die zusammenlebten
Im Gedächtnis, und nicht den Sand nur oder
Die Weiden es hinwegnimmt und die Tempel
Ergreifft, wenn die Ehre
Des Halbgotts und der Seinen
Verweht und selber sein Angesicht
Der Höchste wendet
Darob, dass nirgend ein
Unsterbliches mehr am Himmel zu sehn ist oder
Auf grüner Erde, was ist dies?

Christopher Middleton catches much of the parasyntactic whirl and crossfire of the original:

But when he dies then
To whom beauty
      Most clung, making his form
Flesh of a miracle
      And the powers of heaven
Pointed to him, and when, eternally
      Riddles to one another, they
      Cannot grasp one another, who
Lived as one
   In memory, and when it takes away
Not the sand only, nor the willows,
      When it takes hold
   Of the temples, when the demigod
And his own are all
      Stript of honor, and even the Highest
Averts his gaze, whence not a shred
      Of immortality is seen in heaven or on

The green earth, what is this?

Even Middleton's admirable version domesticates Hölderlin's torrent: tames the tumble of clauses with added punctuation, corrals the lunge and yaw of the syntax more quickly than does the original. Still, the forward/lateral action is unmistakable.

*

As the German demonstrates, Hölderlin appears to have arrived at free scoring a hundred years before Pound. But we'll set questions of micro-rhythm aside, and focus on what's taking place at the mezzo-scale. Across the whole stanza, the syntax bucks and swivels. The poem moves in a welter of simultaneous energies.

What are these energies?

One answer would be: the ideas Hölderlin is expressing. Because they are complex, the syntax has to be complex to articulate them. But that's not good enough. For a start, the passage doesn't "express ideas." It presents events in the sacred history of the West, in a densely visionary mode. And more than that: if Hölderlin was simply trying to communicate this content, there's no reason he couldn't have organized it more straightforwardly. A copy editor could easily improve the stanza — breaking it into three or four shorter sentences, supplying connectives, and resolving these syntactic air-pockets where we seem to hang in space, propelled in two or three directions at once.

Needless to say, the improvements would gut the poem. Hölderlin himself was taken aback by the music he found himself obeying. But as he declared (in a headnote to "Friedensfeier"), "If some should think such speech too unconventional, I must confess to them: I cannot help it." That is: whatever these energies may consist of, their whiplash dynamics possess a life of their own. Hölderlin's task was to let them play through the poem as cleanly as possible. For at the deepest level, their compound music *was* the poem — sustaining and animating everything else.

This stands as pure kintuition: direct apprehension of a body music that lies beneath or beyond the actual words, and furnishes the rhythms by which they move. If it were not for the composite movement of the poem, we might never know these energies existed. But there they palpably are, commingling in its trajectory.

Calling them "energies" is merely a way of saluting their cosmophonic source. I wish I had a better term to pay it homage. But in any case, this way of moving taps into a rich and plural sonic space — one whose polyrhythms are enacted directly on the page.

43.

What kintuition does compound rhythm bespeak?

It says, there is always *more*. The frequencies of being are a sounding plethora. No matter how mobile the poetic line, the energies that attune it are more multiform, more simultaneous than consciousness can hope to organize. Reality is richer than all of our formulations of reality. And compound rhythm declares this, not by asserting it conceptually, but by enacting it kinaesthetically. In the dangerous rhythms of more.

This is voice with its life on the line. Shipwrecked ekstasis: manifold being, at once.

44.

The source of poetic authority here is not Friedrich Hölderlin. It is the polyrhythmic cadence of what is.

So it is not that everyone else should try to sound like Hölderlin. God spare us another orthodoxy, one more sure-fire technique. The point is that the kinaesthetic space he skidded into, two hundred years ago, is far richer than our current maps recognize. The truest response is not to imitate him, but to attend to the polyrhythmic energy of what is. Given such attending, many different musics can emerge within the syntax of compound rhythm.

To write like Hölderlin today would mean accepting the directive: utter us utterly. With no blueprint for what the poem should sound like.

45.

And I got drunk on that sonic niagara. From my twenties on, Hölderlin and Pindar (in translation; my Greek is too spotty) were my rhythmic *Lear*.

46.

Some features of compound rhythm emerge more clearly if we set it beside free prosody, comparing them as grammars of coherence on different scales.

Scoring syncopates two protocols, both variable; compound rhythm orchestrates unprogrammed energies. That is, neither relies on a fixed measure to calibrate the rhythm.

That said, there appears to be nothing in composite rhythm corresponding to the twin protocols of syntax and notation. Its energies are all over the map. At the mezzo-scale, the counterpoint of forward/lateral action does not unfold within a binary framework.

The specifically modern innovation in prosody was the shift from fixed/variable to variable/variable. Has there been a comparable change in compound rhythm? You can find forward/lateral movement in classical verse; think of *Paradise Lost*. But has its nature changed in modern practice? Or is the difference chiefly that compound rhythm now draws on free prosody, rather than meter?

I don't have clarity on this question. But as a poet, I'm not particularly concerned to figure it out. What takes precedence is the sheer fact of polyrhythm, which issues its luminous perpetual directive.

Both scoring and compound rhythm give poets room to improvise in whatever key they're drawn to. That is, neither is tied to a single audition of coherence. Each furnishes a syntax for many kinds of body music; each lets us score the rhythmic harmonics in a multitude of ways.

And in fact, forward/lateral action has been practised in varying forms by a wide range of modern poets — none of whom sounds like Hölderlin, or like the others. I think of poets as different as William Carlos Williams, Robert Creeley, Al Purdy, Ed Dorn, Gerald Stern, Don McKay, to name just a handful. It would be a treat to trace the varieties of compound rhythm in their work, though it would take more space than I can devote to it here.

47.

So it is not that we lack precedents for modern mezzo-polyrhythm. But our poetics ignore the precedents that are already there. Our map of the modern continuum leaves crucial rhythms inaudible; it screens out the primacy of body music by ignoring so much of its basic language.

We've got to ventilate this place.

48.

In Hölderlin's poetry, it's the structure of the sentence that is constantly getting recast. His compound rhythms exert their pressure chiefly on the syntax; other dimensions of the poem are much less affected. We could compare him to a jazz soloist who improvises on the melody, but keeps to the original time signature, and plays with a uniform timbre.

That's one way of doing forward/lateral action, and it has the authority of origin. But the clash and convergence of energies can unfold in other dimensions as well.

49.

One such dimension is *voice*. The energies that enter the poem can splay the syntax; they can also roughen or pucker or deepen the tonality. The poem will then register their presence as a series of shifting phonic disturbances. And the trajectory of the poem will be naturally polyphonic.

On the page, these different voices emerge consecutively. But when the poem unfolds as a play of interactive energies, they arise within the larger dance of simultaneity. And we start to hear them not just in sequence, but as overtones.

Polyrhythm expresses itself both in syntactic richness and in polyphony.

50.

And *this* is what I've been pressing to articulate. How technique reaches out, in desire, to recreate the polyrhythms of being.

51.

Honouring polyrhythm leads to a sense of structure which is many-centred, relativist, yet open to the claim of presence. If and when it comes through.

52.

For decades after 1915, it seemed as though "modern poetry" and "modernist poetry" were one and the same. As though the rhythms of Pound and his peers defined the entire sound-scape of a post-classical cosmos. But time has passed, and there's no need to prolong such tunnel audition.

In the 1800s, mathematicians realized that Euclidean space was not the only kind of space that could be conceived. But they didn't declare Riemann's new geometry definitive, nor Lobachevsky's, nor any other single alternative. All were legitimate, though some would prove more fruitful than others.

By the same token, it does not belittle the modernists to observe that their intuitions of a new rhythmic continuum are not the only ones that apply. Nor even, in some cases, the most fruitful. Their legacy is still staggering.

53.

As a thumbnail summary:

At the micro-scale, the creation of scoring was a seminal achievement. Syntax-and-notation may furnish the prosody of English poetry for centuries to come — as metrical prosody did in its time.

At the mezzo-scale, the craft of compound rhythm has been largely ignored in modern poetics. But while our poetics are inadequate as a result, the craft itself has been practised by modern poets in a wide variety of ways.

At the macro-scale, the syntax of rhythm devised by Pound was that of parataxis, or discontinuous form — "vorticism," as he termed it. The basic technique was one of jump-cut ellipsis between "rhyming subjects" (in Hugh Kenner's phrase): between members of a governing analogue class. This provided an alternative to classical, linear logics for relating parts within the whole.

Pound's approach to macro-rhythm has been adopted by many modern poets, and analyzed extensively by critics. It is my conviction that as a syntax of major form, it engenders problems which it cannot resolve. However the subject is so far-reaching that I won't try to address it here.

54.

If polyrhythmic form is many-centred and relativist, it has a lot in common with the impulses of postmodernism. The latter rejects the Olympian perspective of modernism; it talks about disrupting master narratives, destabilizing unitary systems of meaning, revalorizing the margins. And that is an admirable job description.

Yet in practice I find myself restless. Not with the project itself, but with the spirit in which it is often promoted. For a great deal of its discourse goes on within a skewy ontophony.

What leads me to balk is the assumption that decentring monolithic systems is an achievement of postmodern thinkers and artists. Or that it's a human activity at all. In terms of power politics, of course, that's precisely what it is. Every authorized system renders the truths of the marginalized invisible; reclaiming those truths demands a dedicated energy of subversion. But that said, the fact is that *we* can't decentre the stories. They're already decentred. Polyrhythm precedes us; being is plural, with or without our permission. And the appropriate first response is not parody, nor even struggle, but awe. For polyrhythm is not a human creation. To think otherwise is hubris.

This blinkered ontophony has led to the shallow gamesmanship that vitiates so much postmodern poetry and fiction, and to the recombinant jargon of so much cultural theory. Its perpetual de-ing and dissing can become a refuge; it can be safer to spin theories about polyphasic meaning than to head out and try to honour its cataclysmic demands.

No recipes; no nets.

55.

How to live in the here and now, with only variable meanings to go on?

You can spend your energy exposing how particular words fail to signify what is. Or you can wait upon what it is that words will always fail to signify.

56.

What is rhythm?

Or rather: what are simultaneous rhythms, when none is master, privileged, normative? For the body music of world *is* many-centred. What is at issue is the nature of its relativity.

It is reductive relativism to conclude that the truth of A is explained away or cancelled because it fails to include the truths of B and C. For B and C are inevitably subject to the same dismissal, till finally all that remains is the clever smirk of the dismisser.

Yet we have no choice; we have to be relativist through and through. There is nothing we apprehend that doesn't get filtered through our personal temperament and cultural codes. But recognizing that has nothing to do with reductionism. Two things are true at once: we limit and distort what claims us; and we *are* claimed. Neither truth is enough without the other.

It is polyrhythmic relativism to honour the simultaneous play of A and B and C. Sustained, as they are, in cadence — painfully at times, in what feels like a numinous relativity. A holy.

*

But how do you honour these jostling frequencies when fixed measures are gone? How do you enact a coherence-in-motion which is local, provisional, unstable, renewable, in-process?

By waiting, beholden, on cadence. Rich polyrhythmic manifold.

57.

When you absorb rhythm kinaesthetically, the classic Western split between subject and object goes into remission.

It survives, in a weakened sense. But the old, unbridgeable distance of over-against is largely bad rhythm now. Bad ontophonic grammar.

For you are just not a self-contained subject/observer — you're embedded in kinaesthetic space. And when you register its frequencies, what configures you is both outside you and within. You're a subset, a local constituent: one swatch of the plural whole. Now subject and object unclench, subside to secondary distinctions within the field.

I don't experience this as a total whiteout of ego. The local *I* goes on. But the wrench and plash and momentum go on too, and oneself is included — well before deliberate listening even begins. You could bar the door, but the walls are already down.

What is it you hear? I don't know if I'm talking about stones in a field or the sacred. All I know is, kintuition goes there. Polyrhythm is true.

58.

Body music is the mind of poetry. Its rhythms think who we are, and what the world is. Not exhaustively, for there are other ways of thinking. But for real.

Kinaesthetic polyrhythm is one alternative to the impasse of modern reason — to the inability of technical thought to know the world, except by shrinking it to its own value-free categories. Polyrhythm thinks beneath the impasse, within the impasse, beyond the impasse.

★

But is it not a fresh act of hubris, to put forward a poet's experience of cadence as a paradigm of other-than-modern knowing?

Au contraire. Many kinds of witness are needed. And while this is not the only non-modern way of knowing — who will speak for it, if I don't?

Just as, if others don't tell us what *they've* been claimed by, who will?

Notes on the Text

All the essays have been revised since their last publication.

"Cadence, Country, Silence" began as a ten-minute presentation at the third annual "Rencontre québécoise internationale des écrivains" in Montreal in 1972. An incomplete version was published in *Liberté*, 14, No. 6 (1972). It then appeared in *Open Letter*, Ser. 2, No. 6 (Fall 1973); *boundary 2*, 3, No. 1 (Fall 1974); and later reprintings.

A version of "Roots and Play" was delivered at the Loughborough International Seminar on Canadian children's literature, held in Toronto in August 1975. It was published in *Canadian Children's Literature*, No. 4 (1976). Some of the poems included here were written subsequently.

"Polyphony" began as an interview conducted by Jon Pearce in 1978. A rewritten version appeared as "Enacting a Meditation" in the *Journal of Canadian Poetry*, 2, No. 1 (Winter 1979). That served as a basis for the present essay, published in *Descant*, No. 39 (Winter 1982).

"The Poetry of Al Purdy" appeared as the Afterword to *The Collected Poems of Al Purdy* (McClelland & Stewart, 1986). Quotations are from that volume. Used by permission of the author.

"Acts of Dwelling, Acts of Love" was published in the *Globe and Mail* on August 26, 1989. The epigraphs at the beginning and end are from *The Stubborn Particulars of Grace* (McClelland & Stewart, 1987). The poem is from *Common Magic* (Oberon, 1985); used by permission.

"Judy Merril Meets Rochdale College" was printed in *Aloud*, 2, No. 7 (October 1992), as part of a tribute to Judith Merril during the International Festival of Authors at Harbourfront, Toronto.

"Memories of Miron" appeared in *Liberté*, 39, No. 5 (October 1997), in a translation by Marie-Andrée Lamontagne. The English version was published in *Brick, A Literary Journal*, No. 60 (Summer 1998).

"Grant's Impasse" was delivered at a 1989 conference on George Grant at Carleton University, and published in *By Loving Our Own* (Carleton University Press, 1990).

"The Luminous Tumult" is based on a 1993 interview conducted by Donna Bennett and Russell Brown. It appeared in *Poetry Canada Review*, 14, No. 2 (1994).

"Poetry and Unknowing" draws on an interview by Michael Higgins, Peter Hinchcliffe, and John Porter, published in *The New Quarterly* (Summer 1994). It was recast for *Poetry and Knowing* (Quarry, 1995), a volume of essays edited by Tim Lilburn.

"Body Music" began as a background paper for a colloquium on "Dennis Lee and Canadian Literary Polyphony," held at Trent University in 1996. This version was written in 1998. The Hölderlin translation is from Christopher Middleton, *Friedrich Hölderlin, Eduard Mörike: Selected Poems* (University of Chicago Press, 1972), © 1972 by the University of Chicago. All rights reserved.